Math Art + Drawing Games for Kids

40+ Fun Art Projects to Build Amazing Math Skills

KARYN TRIPP

QUARRY

To Rich, Brennan, Elise, and Burton
for helping make this possible.

Quarto.com

© 2020 Quarto Publishing Group USA Inc.

Text and Projects © 2020 Karyn Tripp

Photography © 2020 Karyn Tripp

First Published in 2019 by Quarry Books, an imprint of The Quarto Group,

100 Cummings Center, Suite 265-D, Beverly, MA 01915, USA.

T (978) 282-9590 F (978) 283-2742

Quarry Books titles are also available at discount for retail, wholesale, promotional, and bulk purchase. For details, contact the Special Sales Manager by email at specialsales@quarto.com or by mail at The Quarto Group, Attn: Special Sales Manager 100 Cummings Center, Suite 265-D, Beverly, MA 01915, USA.

10 9 8 7

ISBN: 978-1-63159-769-5

Digital edition published in 2020

eISBN: 978-1-63159-770-1

Library of Congress Cataloging-in-Publication Data is available

Design and page layout: Laura McFadden Design, Inc.

Photography: Karyn Tripp

Printed in USA

Acknowledgments

Writing this book has been such a fun learning process. I have always wanted to write a book, so it is a dream come true. It was harder than I expected, and I could not have done it without the support of those closest to me. I want to take a moment to say thank you!

I want to start by thanking my husband, Rich, for supporting me throughout this process and giving up all his weekends to take the kids while I worked. I love you for your selflessness! You are my rock.

I want to thank my mom for helping me with the brainstorming and the babysitting! Thanks for encouraging me to be myself and to explore my talents. Thanks for giving me a bit of your creative talent and for teaching me all you know.

To my dad, thanks for helping me learn how to dream big and not be afraid to follow my dreams. Thank you for many years of support and love.

Thanks to my amazing mother-in-law, who was also a huge help with the kids during this process. I could not have done it without you.

My four kids, Brennan, Elsie, Burton, and Millie, are the reason all of this has happened. Teaching them all these years has given me knowledge and courage to do hard things. It has given me confidence that I am smart enough, I am creative enough, and I am brave enough. They put up with all my projects and experiments as the testers to make sure they are fun enough and not too complicated. Love to all four of you. You make my life better.

To my blog followers: You are all amazing, and I thank you for your support all these years. Your notes of encouragement and thanks keep me going. I love creating for you!

Thanks to the awesome team at Quarto. You have been so great to work with and have helped me figure out this process. Thanks for being patient with me as I learn how to write a book.

One last thank-you goes to my Learning Circle ladies. This group of my dearest friends helps me through the hard days that come all too often. They encourage me and ground me.

CONTENTS

3   Acknowledgments

7   Introduction

8   What You'll Need

11   Key Math Concepts

1 = Math with Fine Artists 14

Fine artists often use math in their creations. Explore their artwork with these fun projects.

16   Paul Klee's Geometric Mosaic

18   M. C. Escher's Infinity Triangles

20   Victor Vasarely's Op Art Illusions

22   Alexander Calder's Face Mobile

24   Frank Stella's Protractor Art

26   Jasper Johns's Hidden Number Art

28   Frank Lloyd Wright's Geometric
      Stained-Glass Art

2 = Art with Graphs & Grids, Numbers & Equations 30

Try creative mathematical projects on graph paper, and count your way through art with projects that feature equations.

32   Square Numbers Tower

34   Dot Grid Art

36   Multiplication Grid Art

38   Skip Counting Circular Art

40   Golden Spiral Art

42   Splash Patterns

44   Vedic Square

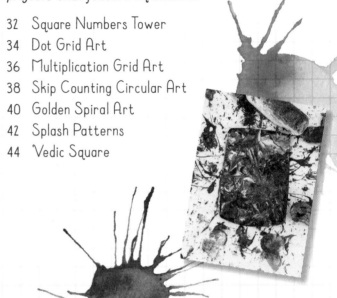

3 = Symmetry in Art 46

Symmetry is when two or more parts are identical on either side of a shape or form. Explore these fun ways to make art with symmetry.

48   Rotational Symmetry

50   Paper Clip Symmetrical Art

52   Mandala Drawings

54   Kirigami Paper Cutting

56   Rose Window Stained Glass

58   Hectograph Ink Prints

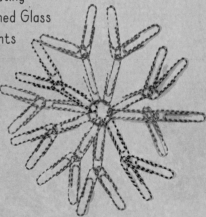

4 = Geometric Art 60

Get creative with shapes and lines.

62 Spiral Squares
64 Descending Polygons
66 Triangle Math Puzzle
68 3-D Paper Shapes
70 Tetrahedral Kite

6 = Edible Math Art 88

Everything is always more fun when food is involved. The projects in this section are all edible. You're welcome!

90 Pattern Block Cookies
92 Waffle Fraction Patterns
94 Chocolate Square Splatter Art
96 Bread Art: Doubling a Recipe
98 Stained Glass Gelatin Art

5 = Cultural Math Art 72

Art has been created throughout history and around the world. And in most art, math and patterns are involved.

74 Native American Quill Art
76 African Kente-Pattern Prints
78 Buddhist Sand Pendulum Art
80 Spanish Geometric Tile Cube Puzzles
82 Ancient Cretan Labyrinth
84 Islamic Eight-Pointed Stars
86 Yin-Yang Asian Geometrical Art

More Stuff

100 Templates
111 Resources
111 About the Author
112 Index

Introduction

When I was young, math was my hardest subject, but I did love art. I never realized how much they had in common until later in life.

A Note for Parents & Teachers

I really did not like math at first. I remember crying over it often as a kid. I was so relieved when I was finished taking my last math class in college, thinking I would be finished with it forever! When I started homeschooling my kids, I saw that this would not be the case. It was when my own kids started telling me that they hated math that I really thought hard about how to teach it in new ways. It was important to me that my kids did not have the same feelings about math that I always did.

I started making math into an activity instead of just a worksheet. I came up with games and projects that were engaging so my kids could grasp the harder concepts without tears. It brings me so much joy to help a child delight in learning. Along the way, I fell in love with math.

My biggest hope is that this book can help you do the same with your kids or your students.

There are many opportunities in these projects for kids to be original and innovative. Don't be afraid to let them express themselves in their own artistic ways.

A Note for Kids

We always hear how important it is to know and understand math. It's used in life in so many ways. When you can find a little joy and meaning in math, there's less fear of it. In this book, I teach you different ways it's used in real life. Artists use it in their work, bakers use it in their recipes, and architects use it in their designs. These art projects will help you bring some excitement to your math lessons by getting creative and messy with math!

Math is more than just numbers. Knowing math helps you to create and solve problems. Plus, when you add a creative element to your equations, they will be more meaningful and memorable.

This book is geared towards kids ages 8 to 12. I have two kids in that age range, and they did each project along with me as I worked on this book. It made me smile to see how much fun they had.

The most important thing I want to you understand from this book is that math really and truly can be enjoyable. So get ready to have fun and create some amazing art!

What You'll Need

Here are a few of the supplies you'll want to have on hand as you explore this book.

Basic Art and Craft Supplies

- Pencils
- Rulers
- Markers
- Colored pencils
- Paints, acrylic and tempera, along with paintbrushes and jars of water

- Tape
- Compass
- Protractor
- Various sizes and colors of paper
- Graph paper
- Colored tissue paper
- Scissors

- Glue
- Oil and chalk pastels
- Colored jumbo paper clips
- Safety pins
- Corkboard and push pins
- Metal brads
- Toothpicks
- Straws

- Yarn
- Cardboard
- Needles
- Pipe cleaners

Specialty Supplies

- Embroidery thread
- Plastic water bottle
- Polymer clay
- Clay finishing glaze (optional)
- Foam craft sheets
- Wire
- Rocks
- Pine cones
- Colored sand
- Wooden cubes
- Old metal baking sheet
- Glycerin
- Clear contact paper
- Paint roller
- Marble
- Clear suction cups
- Wooden dowels
- Chopsticks

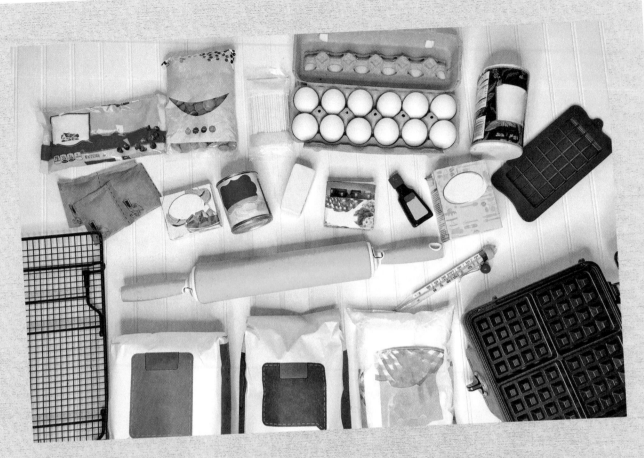

Baking Supplies

- Flour
- Sugar
- Baking soda
- Baking powder
- Salt
- Gelatin (several flavors)
- Unflavored gelatin
- Vanilla extract
- Gel food coloring

- Sweetened condensed milk
- Chocolate
- Colored candy melts
- Chocolate chips, raisins, blueberries, or other small food items
- Waffles or waffle iron
- Butter
- Yeast
- Eggs
- Whipped cream

- Corn syrup
- Maple syrup
- Chocolate molds
- Baking sheets
- Cooling rack
- Rolling pin

Key Math Concepts

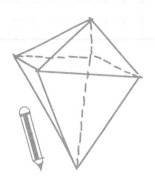

Throughout this book, we'll be talking about several key math concepts. You'll see some of the following terms in the "Math in Action" lists and project instructions. Here's what they mean!

Addition: Determining the total of two or more numbers. For example, 1 + 3 = 4.

Angles: The spaces between intersecting lines. They're usually measured in degrees.

Area: How much space a surface takes up. For example, to find the area of a rectangle, multiply the length by the width. To find the area of a triangle, multiply the base by the height and then divide it by 2.

Balance: Evenly distributed weight. When something is balanced, both of its sides will have the same mass or quantity.

Concentric circles: A series of circles that share the same center but are different sizes.

Coordinate plane: A grid with two intersecting perpendicular number lines. It is used to plot points with x and y coordinates.

Counting: Starting at a number and increasing it or decreasing it by the same amount every time. For example, to determine the number of items in a group, you can count them.

Diameter of a circle: The length of a straight line passing through the center of a circle.

Dimensions: Length, depth, and width. A two-dimensional (or flat) object has two dimensions, and a three-dimensional object has all three.

Fraction: Part of a number, written with one number on top of another. The top number says how many parts there are, and the bottom number says how many equal parts the whole is divided into. Example: ¼. The whole is divided into four parts, and we have one of them.

Geometry: A branch of math that deals with lines, solids, points, and their relationships to each other. It also covers flat and three-dimensional shapes.

Golden ratio: Often found in geometry, art, and architecture, the golden ratio appears when the longer part of something divided by the smaller part is equal to the whole length divided by the longer part. This number is approximately 1.62.

Graph: A set of points that shows an exact position. On graphs it is usually a pair of numbers: the first number shows the distance along an axis, and the second number shows the distance up or down.

Isosceles triangle: An isosceles triangle has two sides of equal length and two equal angles. An isosceles right triangle has one 90° angle and the other two angles are each 45°.

Measurement: The amount or size of something, for example in weight, length, or volume.

Multiplication: Finding out the total when you have a number of sets of some other number. For example, if you have 5 sets of 10: 5 x 10 = 50.

Negative numbers: Numbers less than zero.

Number recognition: The ability to name and identify numerals.

Parallel lines: Lines that extend in the same direction and never cross.

Pattern: A series or a sequence that repeats. It could be in, for example, shapes, colors, or numbers.

Percentage: Parts per 100. The symbol for it is %. For example, 25% means 25 parts per 100.

Perimeter: The distance around a shape. To find it, add the lengths of all the sides together.

Perpendicular lines: Lines meeting at a right angle, or 90°.

Pi: The ratio of a circle's circumference to its diameter, or the measurement around the circle divided by the distance across it. For every circle, it is always the same number, with infinite digits beginning with 3.14. The symbol is π.

Positive numbers: Numbers greater than zero.

Problem solving: Finding the answer to a question.

Proportion: A comparative relation between properties such as size, number, or quantity.

Right triangle: A triangle that has one 90° angle.

Shape: The form of an object. Common two-dimensional shapes include circles, squares, and triangles. Common three-dimensional shapes include spheres, cubes, and pyramids.

Skip counting: Counting forward or backward by a number other than one. For example, counting by 2s: 2, 4, 6, 8, 10 . . .

Spatial ability: Being able to think about objects in three dimensions and picture how they will look rotated or fitting into a space.

Subtraction: Determining the difference between two numbers. For example, 4 – 1 = 3.

Symmetry: When two or more parts of a shape are identical when it's flipped or turned. Rotational symmetry is when the shape looks the same after being rotated. Reflective symmetry is when every part of a shape matches or reflects another across a central point.

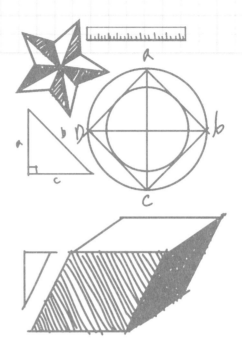

Temperature: How hot or cold something is. It is measured on the Fahrenheit or Celsius scales.

Time: The ongoing sequence of the past, present, and future. It is measured in seconds, minutes, hours, days, weeks, months, and years. We measure it using clocks and calendars.

Weight: How heavy something is. It is the downward force caused by gravity on an object. It is measured in ounces, pounds, and tons in the U.S.; it converts to mass units of grams, kilograms, and tonnes in the metric system.

1

Math with Fine Artists

Mathematics and art. You may think they're more different than alike, but you'd be surprised to see how often they overlap! Both math and art include patterns, shapes and lines, ratios, and proportion. These concepts are incredibly important for both artists and mathematicians.

You've likely seen art with beautiful geometric shapes or with repeating patterns. Without some knowledge of geometry or symmetry, these artists could not create such beauty!

In this chapter, we explore the work of some great artists and use math to re-create some of their works. We use angles and circles, area and perimeter, balance, and lots of color.

Learn about the work of great artists, including M. C. Escher, Wassily Kandinsky, Victor Vasarely, Frank Stella, Alexander Calder, Jasper Johns, Paul Klee, and Frank Lloyd Wright. You can see how they use math in their artwork and why it matters. Have fun creating!

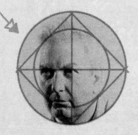

Paul Klee's Geometric Mosaic

Paul Klee (1879-1940) was a Swiss-German artist who worked during the late 1800s and early 1900s. He had a unique style influenced by cubism, impressionism, and surrealism. This project is based on his painting *Castle and Sun*, which is made up of colorful geometric shapes that form a castle. You can create your own piece of art patterned after Klee's painting using pieces of paper.

Math in Action: *geometry, pattern, spatial ability*

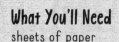

What You'll Need

sheets of paper in several colors

scissors

copy of Paul Klee's painting *Castle and Sun*

glue

1 Cut squares, triangles, and rectangles of various sizes out of several colors of paper.

2 Study Klee's painting *Castle and Sun* for inspiration. Design a shape castle on a large piece of dark-colored paper.

3 Glue on your shapes. You can create any patterns you want. Make it your own!

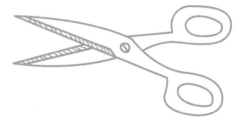

M. C. Escher's Infinity Triangles

Dutch artist M. C. Escher (1898-1972) is famous for his tessellations as well as merging difficult mathematical concepts with art. This project is inspired by his illusions of infinity. He created many pieces of art that illustrate a view of something extending on forever. Here we illustrate it in a simpler way with triangles.

Math in Action: *geometry, measurement*

What You'll Need

ruler

pencil

colored construction paper

scissors

larger piece of construction paper

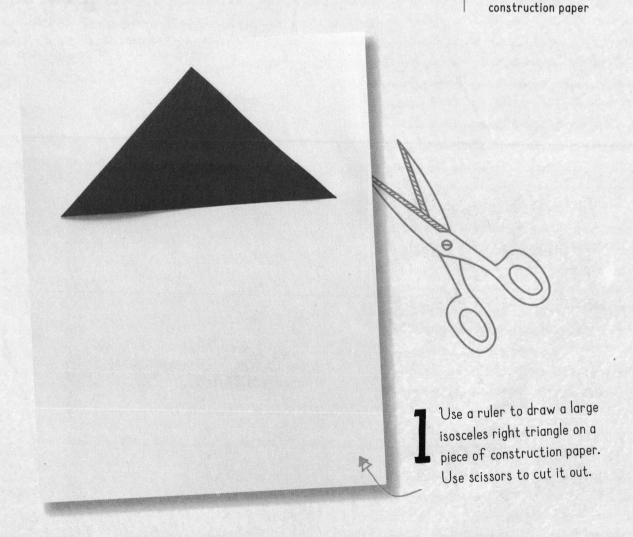

1 Use a ruler to draw a large isosceles right triangle on a piece of construction paper. Use scissors to cut it out.

2 Make two more of the same shape triangles, each in a different color, but smaller: the short, equal sides of your new triangles should be the same length as half of the long side of the first triangle. They'll end up each being half the area of the larger triangle, too. Arrange the three triangles on the larger piece of paper to make a square. Continue this pattern, cutting four triangles that are each half the area of the previous two. Arrange them on the paper.

3 Repeat with four triangles each half the area of the two facing the bottom of your design, as shown. Repeat again with eight triangles half again as small. For the next row, you will need eight small triangles half the area of those in the previous row and sixteen half again as small. This pattern can continue into infinity, or until you can't cut triangles any smaller!

Victor Vasarely's Op Art Illusions

Victor Vasarely (1906-1997) was a French-Hungarian artist known for starting the op art movement. Op art is an abstract art style that looks like an optical illusion. The patterns and shapes create movement and often look three-dimensional. Try creating your own op art!

Math in Action: *geometry, parallel lines, shape*

What You'll Need

paper

pencil

ruler

markers

compass

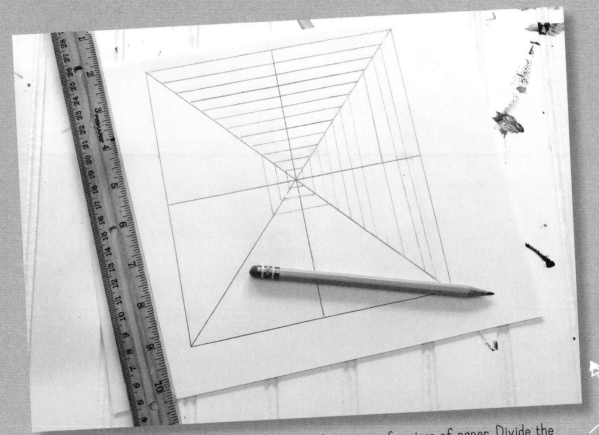

1 To make an op art square, draw a large square in the center of a piece of paper. Divide the square into eight equal triangular pieces by using a ruler to draw lines from corners to corners and across the middle both ways. Using the ruler again, draw ten to twelve lines across each triangular section. Make sure the lines match up with the lines in the sections next to them.

2 Color the lines in an alternating pattern, as shown.

3 Try again with a circle in the center. Or try covering your paper with lots of smaller squares as shown. To make a 3-D circle, draw a circle in the center of the paper. Using a ruler, draw a checkerboard pattern on the rest of the paper. Inside the circle, match up the lines at the edges, but use a compass to make them curved instead of straight. This will make the circle look like it's coming out of the paper! Color it in.

Alexander Calder's Face Mobile

Alexander Calder (1898-1976) was a twentieth-century American artist famous for his kinetic sculptures and mobiles. He did a lot of work with balance and movement. He thought art was too static; he loved creating pieces with the potential for movement! In this project, you'll create your own Calder-inspired mobile and test different balance points. It's based on Calder's sculpture *Little Face*.

Math in Action: *balance, dimensions, proportion, symmetry, weight*

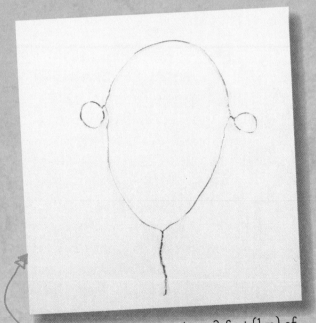

1 Measure out and cut about 3 feet (1 m) of wire. Bend it into the shape of a head and twist the ends together at the bottom. Twist the sides of the head to create ears.

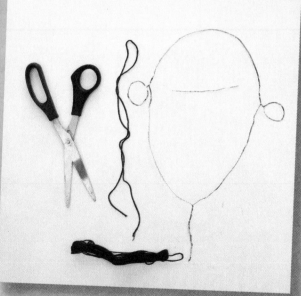

2 Cut a small piece of wire (a few inches [cm] long) to hang the eye pieces from. Use embroidery thread to hang the wire from the top of the head.

3 Cut a nose and a mouth out of craft foam. Poke a hole through each and thread them onto a piece of embroidery thread to keep them secure. Hang them from the center of the wire.

4 Poke a hole in the top of each suction cup and thread embroidery thread through it. Twist the thread around the center pieces of the suction cups and tie to secure. Hang the suction cups on either side of the nose and mouth as eyes.

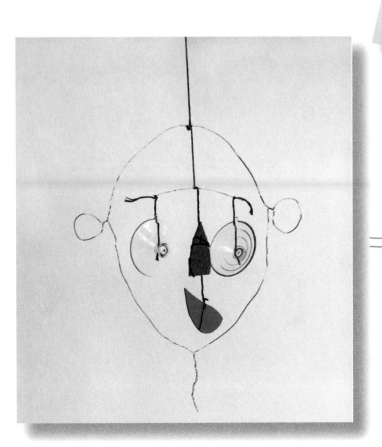

5 Put a dab of glue on each knot to keep the pieces from sliding around on the wire. Once the glue is dry, hang your head from a long piece of string.

Frank Stella's Protractor Art

This project is based on *Takht-i-Sulayman Variation I*, an artwork by Frank Stella (1936-), from his Protractor series. Stella has created more than 100 paintings based on the shape of a protractor. Get out your protractor and get ready to create beauty with it!

Math in Action: *angles, geometry, measurement*

What You'll Need

protractor

paper

pencils

oil pastels or other coloring supplies

1 Use a protractor to create your design. Start by tracing the outer and inner edges onto your paper.

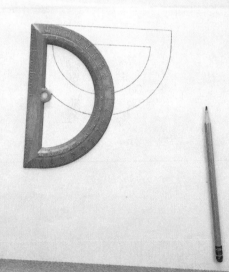

2 Turn the protractor 90 degrees as shown, matching up the corner with the corner of the first one you traced. Trace the outer and inner edges again.

3 Continue turning and tracing a total of four times. You'll make a square with the curved edges of the protractor facing inward.

4 Color in the shapes you created with oil pastels.

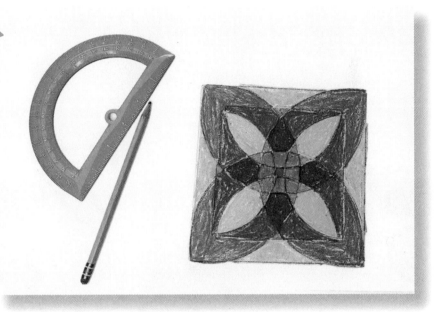

More Shapes and Angles: Vasily Kandinsky

Kandinsky (1866-1944) was a twentieth-century abstract artist from Russia who created art using angles and shapes. Using his painting *Composition 8* as your inspiration, use your protractor plus a compass, ruler, and small bottle caps and other circular items to draw and trace a variety of geometric shapes—lines, circles, semicircles, arcs, and so on—then use crayons or oil pastels to color and decorate them. Try shading and blending shapes that overlap one another.

Jasper Johns's Hidden Number Art

Jasper Johns (1930-) is an American artist known for pop art and abstract expressionism. He created a fun painting involving numbers titled *Abstract Number Art* that inspired this project.

Math in Action: *counting, number recognition*

What You'll Need

a copy of Jasper Johns's *Abstract Number Art*

large pieces of white paper

tempera paints

number templates

black marker

glue

1 Observe the painting *Abstract Number Art* by Jasper Johns to get inspiration. Paint a piece of paper with several patches of color; let dry. Use a black marker to draw or trace large printouts of the numbers 0 to 9 on top of the dried paint.

2 Cut the numbers out. Glue the numbers on a new piece of paper. Let the glue dry.

3 Paint around the numbers, trying to camouflage them. Let dry.

Frank Lloyd Wright's Geometric Stained-Glass Art

Frank Lloyd Wright (1867-1959) was an American architect. In his buildings, he made some beautiful stained-glass creations. This project is based on some of his stained-glass work. Wright designed the Avery Coonley Playhouse as a kindergarten room and used colorful shapes that suggested balloons, flags, and confetti in its windows. Have fun designing and creating your own Wright-inspired stained-glass art.

Math in Action: *angles, geometry, parallel lines, pattern, perpendicular lines*

What You'll Need

pictures of Frank Lloyd Wright's stained-glass creations

colored cellophane or tissue paper

scissors

clear contact paper

glue

black paint

1 Observe Frank Lloyd Wright's stained-glass pieces. Decide how you want to design your own art piece. Cut various shapes out of cellophane to make up your design.

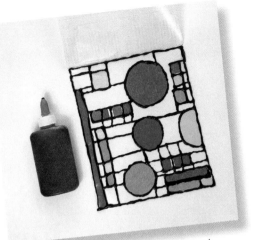

2 Cut out a long, rectangular strip of clear contact paper. Arrange the shapes into your design on half of it. The other half will be folded over once the project is completed.

3 Mix half a bottle of glue with black paint. Shake it well until the glue is black. Use the glue to outline all the shapes and create the leading patterns of the stained glass. Create parallel and perpendicular lines that make right angles as they connect. Let it dry.

4 Fold the other half of the contact paper over your design.

2

Art with Graphs & Grids, Numbers & Equations

Graph paper is paper that's printed with fine lines that make squares, dots, or grids in other shapes. Most often it's used to chart mathematical diagrams, but in this chapter we use graph paper in new ways! The even squares make it easy to measure length and to create symmetry. This allows you to make beautiful patterns and designs without the use of rulers or other tools.

In this chapter, we also explore numbers and equations in fun and interesting ways. You'll solve your way through creative projects with fractions, percentages, skip counting, addition, multiplication, and a whole lot of color.

If you thought math was boring, think again. This chapter will change your mind for good!

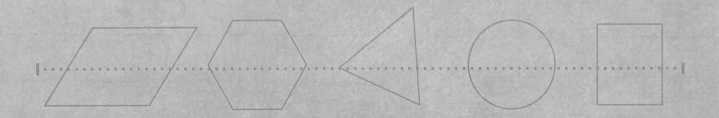

Square Numbers Tower

When a number multiplied by itself, you get a square number. For example, 3 × 3 = 9, so 9 is a square number—3 squared, which is written numerically as 3^2. In this art project, you'll create a graph paper tower by squaring the numbers 1 through 10.

Math in Action: *addition, area, multiplication, perimeter*

What You'll Need

graph paper or colored paper with a graph printed on it

scissors

marker

tape

1 Draw and cut out a large square that is 10 little squares tall and 10 little squares wide. What's the total number of little squares in this large square? Multiply 10 × 10 to figure it out and write your answer in the center. Next, cut out a 9 × 9 square, then an 8 × 8 square. Continue this pattern for each number all the way down to 1.

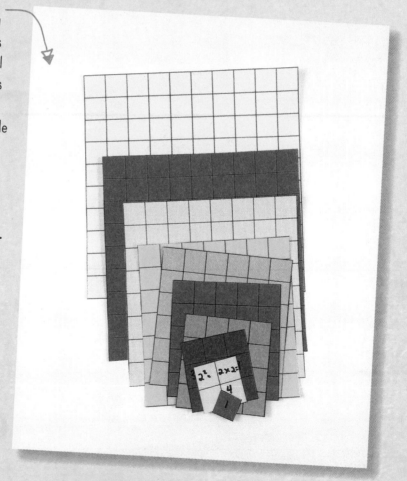

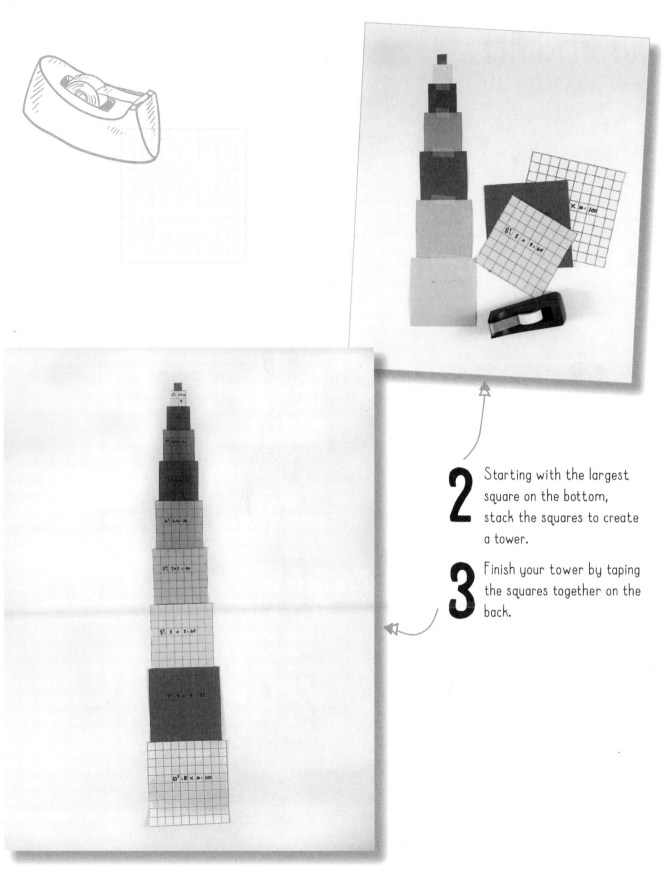

2 Starting with the largest square on the bottom, stack the squares to create a tower.

3 Finish your tower by taping the squares together on the back.

Dot Grid Art

Isometric dot graph paper is a great tool to use to create amazing geometric shapes. This project combines geometry with art to make beautiful pictures!

Math in Action: *area, counting, geometry, perimeter*

What You'll Need

isometric dot
graph paper
(see page 101)

pencil

ruler

markers

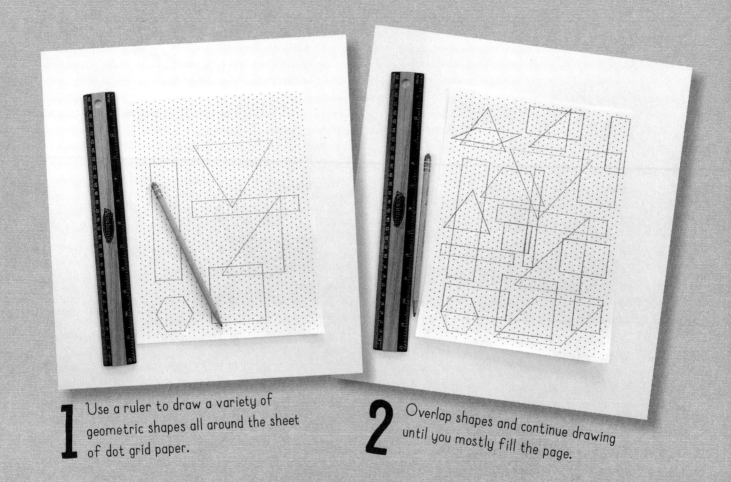

1 Use a ruler to draw a variety of geometric shapes all around the sheet of dot grid paper.

2 Overlap shapes and continue drawing until you mostly fill the page.

3 Color in the shapes. Use a different color each time shapes overlap.

4 Name the types of shapes drawn. Find the area and perimeter of the different shapes.

- To find the area of a square or a rectangle, multiply base × height.
- To find the area of a triangle, multiply base × height, then divide it by 2.
- To find the area of a trapezoid, add together the two different lengths, multiply by the height, and divide by 2.
- To find the perimeter, add the length of each of the sides together.

Multiplication Grid Art

Multiplication can be a lot of fun when you try it in color on graph paper! This is the perfect way to practice your math facts. Let's see how colorful you can make your math.

Math in Action: *area, counting, multiplication*

What You'll Need

graph paper

colored pencils or markers

pen

pair of dice

1 Roll the dice. To multiply the two numbers you rolled, draw a rectangle around the area defined by them.

2 For example, if you roll a 5 and a 3, draw a rectangle that is 5 squares long and 3 squares high. Color in the rectangle and count the colored squares to solve the problem. The 5 × 3 example rectangle contains 15 colored squares: 5 × 3 = 15.

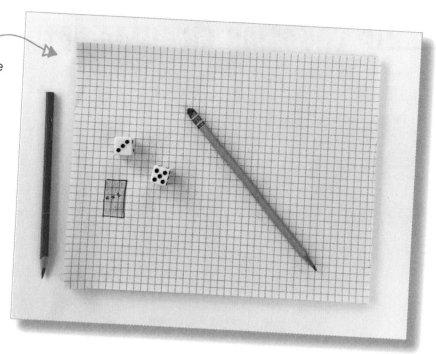

3 Continue rolling, drawing, and coloring. This can be done as a game: Each player takes turns and colors in their own color. The winner has the most area covered at the end.

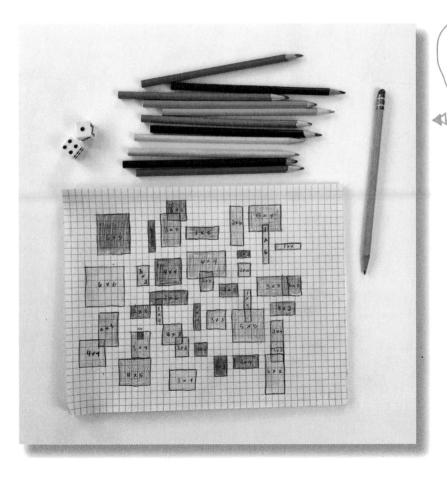

Skip Counting Circular Art

Practice skip counting and your multiplication facts with this fun and colorful multiplication wheel.

Math in Action: *addition, multiplication, skip counting*

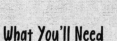

1 Draw a circle and divide it into 12 even sections, or use the template on page 100.

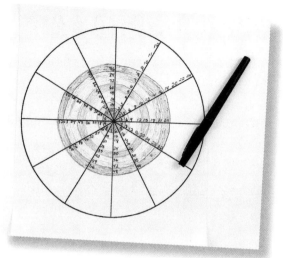

2 Write the numbers 1 to 12 around the center, with one number in each section.

3 In the section with the number 1, fill out the whole section counting by ones to the number 12. In the section with the number 2, do the same, but count by 2s to the number 24. Draw a concentric circle on the outside of each number to create circular rows. Decorate it and color each number row a different color.

4 Continue the pattern, going all the way around the circle.

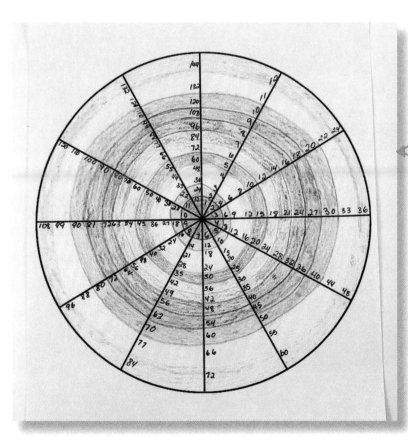

Golden Spiral Art

A golden spiral is made using the golden ratio. You can easily approximate one on graph paper by following the Fibonacci sequence: 0, 1, 1, 2, 3, 5, 8, 13, 21. . . . Each number in the sequence is the sum of the two previous numbers: 1 + 1 = 2, 1 + 2 = 3, 2 + 3 = 5, and so on. In this project, you will use Fibonacci numbers to make beautiful spirals, then turn them into pictures.

Math in Action: *addition, geometry, multiplication*

What You'll Need

graph paper

pencil

ruler

golden rectangle diagrams
(see below)

compass (optional)

markers or other coloring supplies

1 Draw your rectangle using the Fibonacci formula and going in a spiral motion. Use the diagram to the right as a reference. Start by drawing a 13 × 13 square on your graph paper. You can use the ruler or just follow the lines on the graph paper. Connected to that, make a rectangle that is 8 × 13. Divide off an 8 × 8 square, then a 5 x 5 square, a 3 × 3 square, a 2 × 2 square, and 2 squares that are 1 × 1.

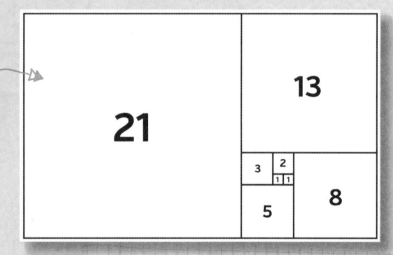

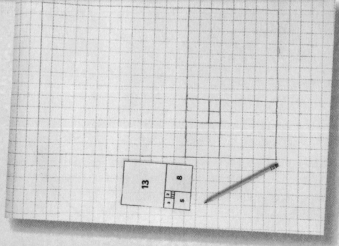

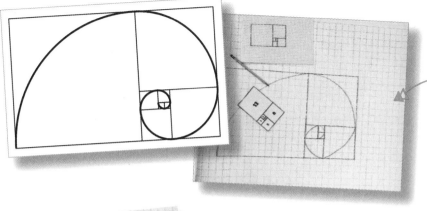

2 Draw a spiral through the entire thing. You can do this using a compass to make it more accurate. Start at the bottom left corner of the largest square and draw a curve to the top right corner. This will connect to the next square. Make a curve across that one and each of the following ones in the same way.

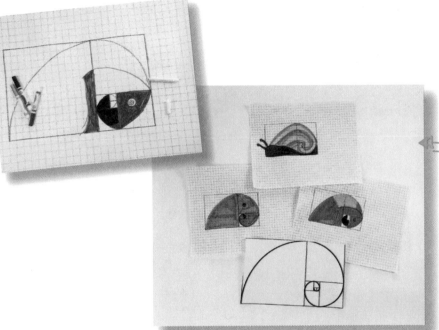

3 Now it's time to get creative and come up with an animal or shape that you want to turn this spiral into. Draw your design and color it in with markers.

Pine Cone Spirals

The Fibonacci sequence can be found throughout nature. One example is the pine cone. If you count the number of spirals in each direction in a pine cone, you'll find a consistent pattern. Start by identifying the different swirls on a pine cone and compare them to the Fibonacci pattern. Paint your pine cone, one spiral for each color. Create beautiful, unique pine cone patterns!

Splash Patterns

This project is messy and tons of fun! Wear clothes and shoes that wash easily or that you don't mind getting a little messy.

Math in Action: *measurement*

What You'll Need

large roll of paper or old newspapers

metal baking sheet or tray

washable paint

rocks

1 Set up for the project. This one gets messy! Roll out paper on the ground outside. Lay a baking sheet on top of it.

2 Fill the pan with paint. The more paint you use, the more fun this project will be.

3 Test different splash patterns by dropping the rocks into the pan of paint. Try dropping them from different heights and angles to see which makes the biggest splashes of paint!

4 Measure the distance of the paint splatters that went the farthest. Which method gave the best result?

Vedic Square

How well do you know your multiplication facts? This project lets you practice that knowledge in a creative way. Once you solve all the problems, you can turn it into a work of art! The Vedic square come from ancient Indian mathematics, and its patterns are seen in Indian and Islamic art.

Math in Action: *addition, geometry, multiplication, pattern*

What You'll Need

blank hundred chart template (see page 102)

paper

pencils

markers

ruler

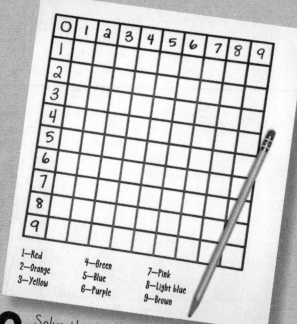

1 Print out a blank hundred chart (see page 102) and gather your other supplies. Number the top row and left column of the chart each from 0 to 9.

2 Solve the multiplication table for 1 to 9. For any two-digit solution, add the two digits together repeatedly until you get a single digit. Fill in all the squares on the chart this way.

1—Red
2—Orange
3—Yellow
4—Green
5—Blue
6—Purple
7—Pink
8—Light blue
9—Brown

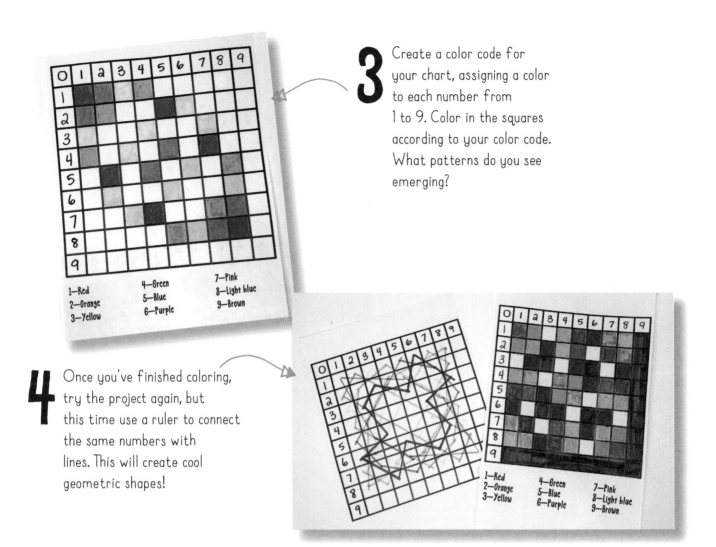

3 Create a color code for your chart, assigning a color to each number from 1 to 9. Color in the squares according to your color code. What patterns do you see emerging?

1—Red
2—Orange
3—Yellow
4—Green
5—Blue
6—Purple
7—Pink
8—Light blue
9—Brown

4 Once you've finished coloring, try the project again, but this time use a ruler to connect the same numbers with lines. This will create cool geometric shapes!

1—Red
2—Orange
3—Yellow
4—Green
5—Blue
6—Purple
7—Pink
8—Light blue
9—Brown

Color by Fractions and Percentages

Another way to use the hundred chart and markers is to use the grid to design patterns and pictures, then determine the fraction or percentage of each color used in your design. You can do this project in two different ways: (1) You can create your design first, then solve the equations; or (2) you can start with a certain percentage and create a design based on that. Figure out the percentage and fraction of each color. For example, if you used a hundred chart and 25 of the squares are colored red, you would say that 25%, or ¼, of the design is red.

3 Symmetry in Art

The word symmetry comes from the Greek words *syn*, meaning "same," and *metros*, meaning "measure." Something has symmetry when it's made up of identical parts facing each other around a central point or across a central line. Symmetry is used in art, in design, and in math. The human brain loves symmetry and is always searching for it in everything we look at. This chapter focuses on projects that have symmetry. There are two main types of symmetry: reflective and rotational. There are examples of both here!

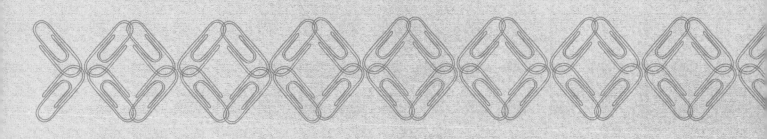

Rotational Symmetry

Rotational symmetry is when something symmetrical rotates around a center point, with multiple identical parts stemming from that point. Examples include a starfish, a flower, and a snowflake. In this activity, you can make your own symmetry by rotating shapes.

Math in Action: *geometry, symmetry*

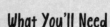

What You'll Need

cardboard

scissors

metal brads

paper or card stock

pencil

coloring supplies

1 Cut a few small shapes out of cardboard. Use a metal brad to attach a shape to the center of a piece of paper or card stock.

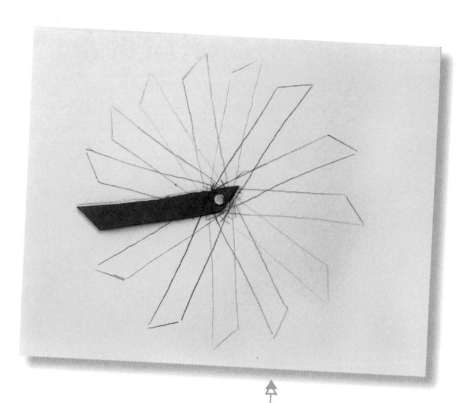

2 Trace the shape. Turn it a small amount and trace it again. Continue turning and tracing all the way around until you reach the beginning.

3 Color and decorate the shapes as desired.

Paper Clip Symmetrical Art

Simple objects such as paper clips can be used to create some amazing symmetrical patterns. This is the perfect activity for a rainy day—grab a bunch of paperclips and start building! Try the shape shown here, then use your own mind to make more shapes and patterns.

Math in Action: *counting, symmetry*

What You'll Need

jumbo paper clips in various colors

keyring or small wire circle

small paper clips in various colors

corkboard and push pins (optional)

1 Attach ten jumbo paper clips to a keyring. Make a color pattern to make it look more interesting.

2 At the end of each one of those paper clips, add two more of the same color, as shown.

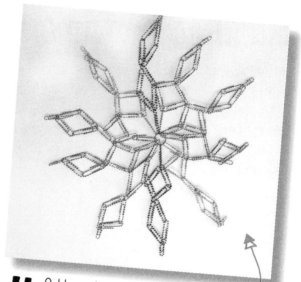

3 Turn each of those pairs into a diamond by adding two more, as shown. Connect each diamond to the one next to it.

4 Add another diamond to each end. Finish each with a single small paper clip.

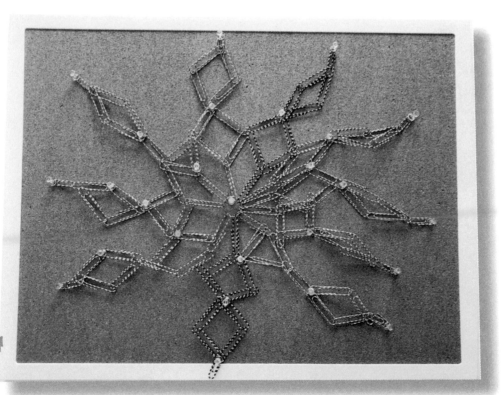

5 To keep it securely in its shape, pin it to a corkboard with push pins. This makes a fun wall decoration!

Mandala Drawings

A mandala is a circular pattern that represents the universe in Hinduism and Buddhism. It is a symbol of wholeness and the cycle of life. Mandalas have been around for thousands of years and come in many shapes and patterns. They include repeating shapes, colors, and patterns starting in the center of the circle and moving outward. Learn to create your own beautiful mandalas in this project. A mandala can be an example of both reflective or rotational symmetry, depending on how you draw it.

Math in Action: *geometry, symmetry*

What You'll Need

paper

compass

pencil

ruler

art supplies for coloring

1 Draw a large circle in the center of the paper with a compass. Draw several more smaller concentric circles within the circle. Divide the circle into several even sections using a ruler. Starting in the center, make a pattern in one small section of the circle. Repeat that pattern around the whole circle or in even sections.

2 Continue creating small patterns within each section until you fill the whole circle with your designs.

3 Color in the patterns.

4 Use the same steps to create another mandala. The possibilities are infinite!

Kirigami Paper Cutting

Kirigami is a style of origami, but it involves cutting the paper as well as folding it. The term *kirigami* comes from the Japanese words *kiri*, which means "cut," and *kami*, which means "paper." This project uses a few simple shapes to make three-dimensional pop-outs.

Math in Action: *concentric circles, geometry, parallel lines, perpendicular lines*

What You'll Need

paper

cutting templates
(see pages 103–105)

scissors

thread or string

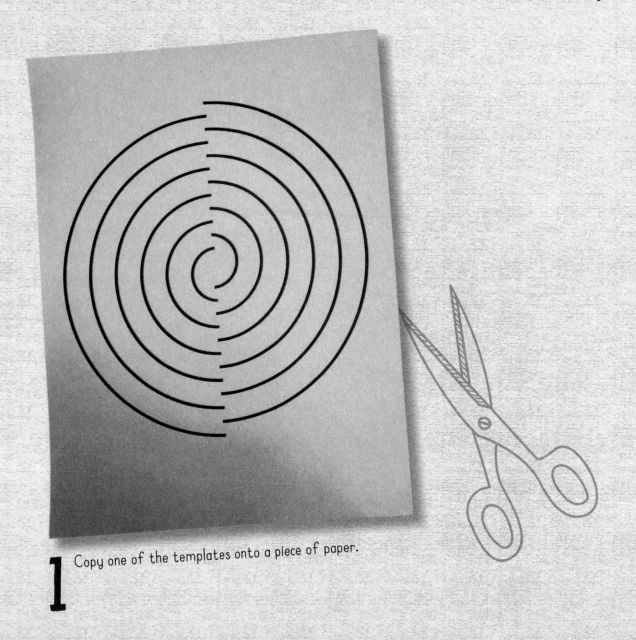

1 Copy one of the templates onto a piece of paper.

2 Fold the shape vertically through the center, where all the lines begin and end. This creates a center dividing line. Unfold, then fold the paper horizontally, matching up the lines on the left side.

3 Cut along the lines on the left side. Unfold. Refold horizontally, matching up the lines on the right side this time. Cut along the lines on the right side.

4 Unfold. Fold each section in alternating directions forward and backward, as shown. Hang by a thread as a decoration.

Rose Window Stained Glass

Rose windows are beautiful stained-glass windows often found in Gothic architecture. They're usually round and divided into symmetrical sections. You can see them in many churches around the world. This project combines the art of the rose window with math through shapes and symmetry.

Math in Action: *geometry, shape, symmetry*

What You'll Need

black construction paper

scissors

colored tissue paper

glue stick

1 Fold together two connecting sides of a piece of black paper, lining up the edges, and trim off the remaining bottom strip to make a square.

2 Keep it folded in half, then fold it in half again.

3 Bring each edge to the center. Trim the bottom edges to make it curved.

4 Cut designs out of the paper as you would on a paper snowflake. Carefully unfold.

5 Cut small pieces of colored tissue paper to fill in the holes. On one side of the black paper, apply glue around the edges of the cutouts and attach the tissue paper. Arrange colors in a symmetrical design.

6 A finished rose window.

Hectograph Ink Prints

A hectograph is a printing method that was developed in the late 1800s. The prefix *hector* comes from the Greek word for "hundred." This process involves preparing a pan of firm gelatin and printing patterns or words with it many times—even 100 times! The fun part about this project is that you can create all kinds of designs to make beautiful art. Repeat patterns with new colors to create symmetry in your artwork.

Math in Action: *measurement, shape, symmetry*

What You'll Need

8 1-tablespoon [7-g] packets plain gelatin

2 cups (0.24 L) glycerin

9 × 13 inch (23 × 33 cm) baking pan or jelly roll pan

large bowl

mixing spoon

washable paint

paint roller

paper

string, scraps of paper, leaves, or any other items to use in your designs

1 Make the gelatin printing plate. In a large bowl, mix together gelatin and glycerin with a mixing spoon. Add 2 cups (0.24 L) very hot water and stir until combined. Pour into a baking pan. Refrigerate to harden for at least 2 hours.

2 Once the gelatin is set, squirt paint on it and use a roller to spread it around.

3 Place string, scraps of paper, leaves, or other items on top of the paint to create your patterns. Use math to create symmetrical patterns and shapes!

4 Place a piece of paper on top of your design and press down. Rub gently and then remove the paper.

5 Set aside to dry.

4 Geometric Art

Geometry and art work together in so many ways. Most people separate art and math as unrelated, but they use very similar skills. Geometry is the study of measurement, lines, angles, shapes, and surfaces. These are also important aspects of art. Artists learn about geometry when learning to draw and use many of the same formulas that a mathematician would use.

Geometry is all around us in the world. Did you know geometry is used in architecture and construction, graphic design and animation, road design, and furniture design? Even athletic fields are designed using geometry! It's definitely an important field of math to understand and learn more about. For this chapter, you'll have fun learning how to use geometry to produce beautiful works of art.

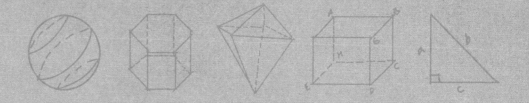

Spiral Squares

This project combines measuring with shapes to make a stunning design. You will use stacks of squares that descend in size and a little glue to make this fun work of art.

Math in Action: *geometry, measurement, shape*

What You'll Need

colored paper

graph paper

ruler

pencil

scissors

glue

1 Draw ten squares in ascending sizes. Make each one ½ inch (1 cm) larger than the previous one. An easy way to do this is by using a piece of graph paper as a template.

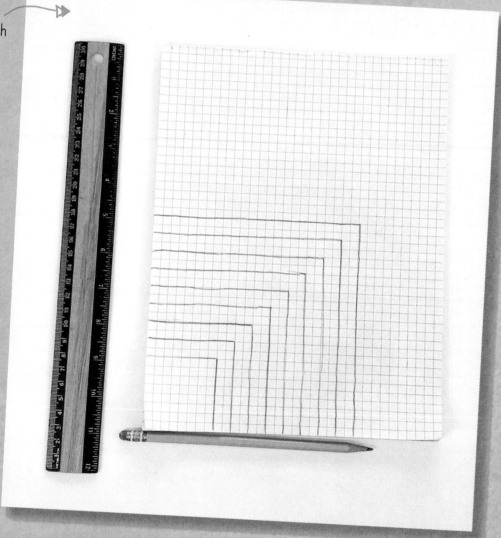

Try This!

Explore this project using other shapes to see if it will work the same way.

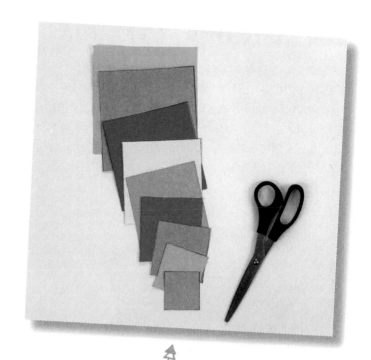

2 Cut out the squares and stack them in different ways to create geometric patterns. To make the patterns more interesting, use a variety of colors.

3 Glue them together in one of the patterns you create.

Descending Polygons

A polygon is a shape or figure with at least three straight sides and angles. The polygons we will use in this project are a triangle (three sides), a quadrilateral (four sides), a pentagon (five sides), a hexagon (six sides), a heptagon (seven sides), an octagon (eight sides), a nonagon (nine sides), and a decagon (ten sides).

Math in Action: *angles, area, geometry, measurement, perimeter*

What You'll Need

paper

ruler

pencil

colored pencils or other art supplies

scissors

stapler, optional

protractor

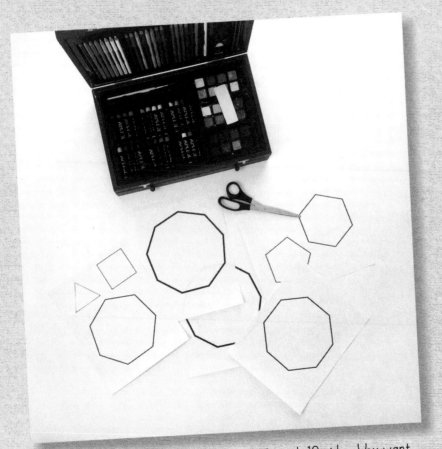

1 Print out or draw polygons with 3 through 10 sides. You want them to all have the same size sides. If they do, the triangle will be the smallest, and the shapes will get gradually larger as the number of sides goes up.

2 Color them each a different color and cut them out.

3 Stack the shapes from smallest to largest. You can staple them together if you like.

Try This!

Label the shapes and measure to find the perimeter of the sides and the area of each one. Use a protractor to measure the angles inside each side.

Triangle Math Puzzle

This colorful project is a game with a beautiful result. We starts with hexagons, which are made up of six triangles, then mix and match them to form a rainbow web of shapes! We add in some math problems to make it even more educational.

Math in Action: *addition, geometry, multiplication*

What You'll Need

colored paper or white paper and colored pencils

hexagon template (see page 106)

scissors

pen

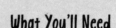

1 Print at least four copies of the hexagon template on colored paper, or print it on white and color it in.

2 Cut out the hexagons.

3 Cut the hexagons into triangles. Write math problems and solutions along the edges of the triangles. It's okay if there are duplicates because it adds to the variety of ways the puzzle can be formed.

4 Match up the edges so problems line up with their solutions to form shapes. You can also match two problems that both have the same solution. Create different patterns. Keep the triangles loose to use them again, or glue them down to save and display your creations.

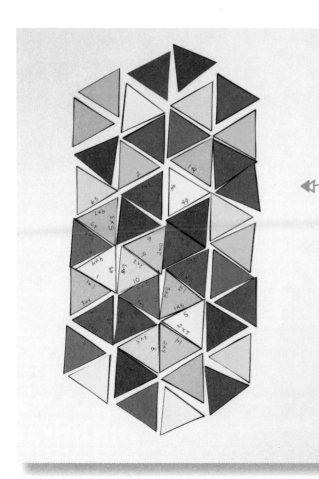

3-D Paper Shapes

Three-dimensional, or 3-D, means an object has height, width, and depth. You can pick it up, touch it, and see all sides of it. Some three-dimensional shapes can be formed and folded from paper. In this project, learn how to make a cone, a cube, a cuboid, a hexagonal prism, a pentagonal prism, square and triangle-based pyramids, and a triangular prism.

Math in Action: *geometry, shape*

What You'll Need

templates (see pages 107-110)

white or colored paper

scissors

coloring supplies, optional

tape

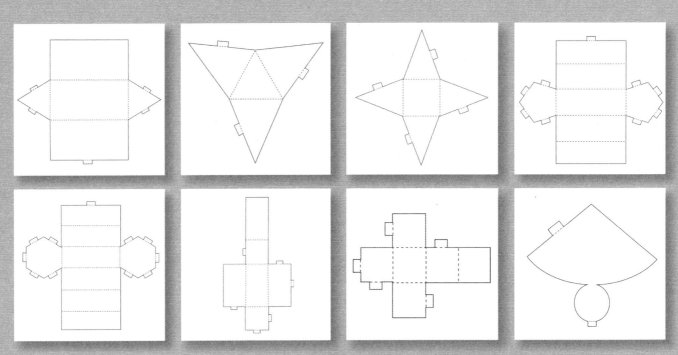

Get larger versions of these templates on pages 107-110.

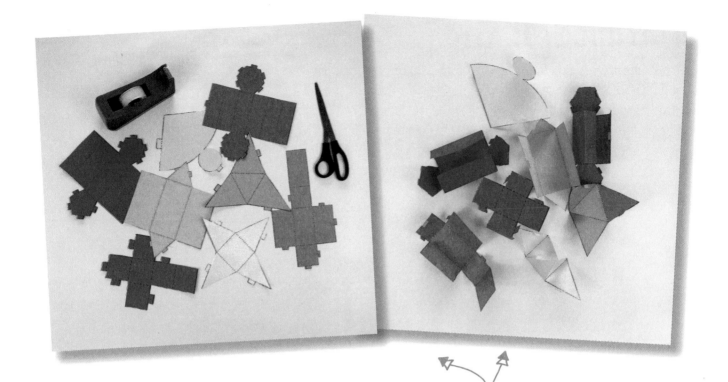

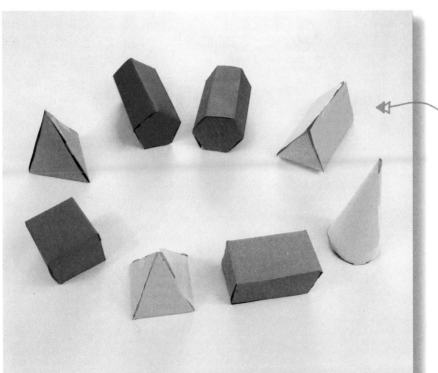

1 Copy the templates and cut them out. If you're using white paper, you can decorate them before assembling the shapes.

2 Fold along the dotted lines and tape the shapes together on the inside to hide the tape.

Try This!

For a more advanced lesson, measure each shape to determine the area, perimeter, and even volume.

Tetrahedral Kite

A tetrahedron is a triangular pyramid. Alexander Graham Bell (1847–1922) once created a giant kite made of 3,393 small tetrahedra that was 40 feet (12 m) long. It could carry a person into the air and was towed by a steamship! The kite in this project is made of small tetrahedrons. When they're assembled, they're in the shape of a tetrahedron.

Math in Action: *geometry, measurement, shape*

What You'll Need

straws

string

tissue paper

scissors

tape

1 Trim the flexible parts off the straws if you're using bendy ones. Thread two 2-foot (0.6 m) pieces of string through one straw.

2 Add two more straws on each string to make two triangles that share a side. Tie the strings at either end to secure.

3 Use the triangles to make a template for the tissue paper, adding flaps on each side to attach the paper to the straws.

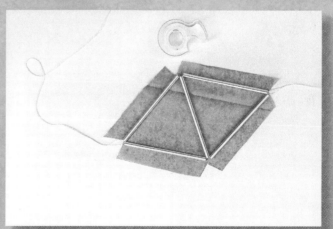

4 Cover three sides of the tetrahedron with tissue paper, folding over the flaps and taping to secure. Add one more straw to close the tetrahedron.

5 Repeat steps 1–4 to make three more tetrahedrons.

6 Attach the tetrahedrons together, with three on the bottom and one on top. Make sure they're all facing the same direction. Tie them together with the strings left hanging from each tetrahedron.

7 Once the tetrahedrons are all attached, tie on a long string that can be used to fly the kite.

Cultural Math Art

Art has been created throughout history and all around the world. The Egyptians used art as their main form of communication. Think of the statue of David created by Michelangelo. He used math to make the proportions of the body just right.

Every culture has different forms of traditional artwork that have long been created and repeated. Art plays an important role in expressing the values and stories of a culture and time period. This chapter explores some of those traditional works of art and, of course, the math involved in making them.

Native American Quill Art

Native Americans use porcupine quills in embroidery and jewelry. The Ojibwe people, for example, are famous for their quill boxes made from birch bark and porcupine quills.

In place of quills, this project uses toothpicks to create art inspired by Native American quill art. The design used is an eight-sided star that's an important symbol to the Sioux people. For them, it's a symbol of immortality and a link between the living and the dead.

Math in Action: *geometry, measurement, symmetry*

What You'll Need

- permanent markers such as Sharpie
- toothpicks
- pencil
- large brown paper
- ruler
- glue

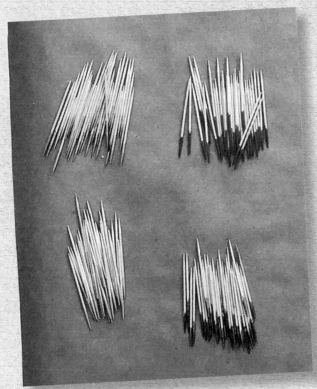

1 Choose four markers in different colors and color the tips of the toothpicks about one-quarter to one-third of the way up. They represent porcupine quills.

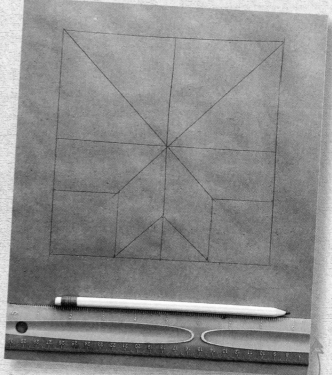

2 Draw a large square in the center of your paper. Use a ruler to divide the square in half four different ways to create an 8-point star as shown.

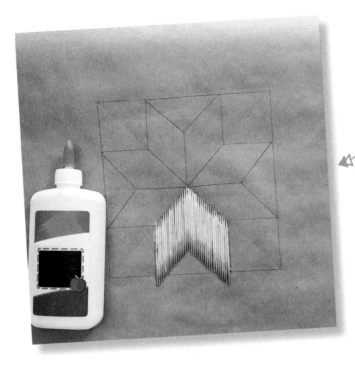

3 In two of the eight points on one side of the star, glue down the toothpicks of one color.

4 Repeat with the toothpicks in the three other colors to complete the star.

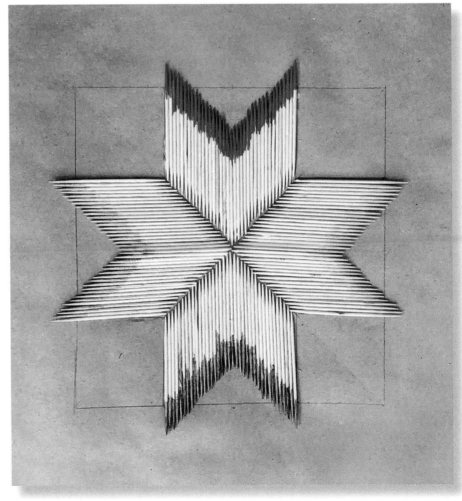

African Kente-Pattern Prints

The word *kente* means "basket" and comes from the West African Ashanti people, who are from what is now known as Ghana. It refers to colorful fabric that was first made from the fibers of a raffia tree and then from silk for royalty. Today kente cloth is made from a variety of colors and patterns, which have meaning and stories behind them. Let it inspire you for this project, in which you'll make your own colorful patterns by creating your own stamps.

Math in Action: *geometry, pattern, symmetry*

What You'll Need

cardboard

scissors

glue

pipe cleaners

craft foam

paint

baking sheet or other large pan

large paper

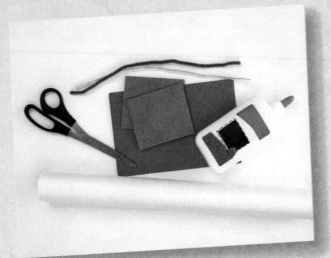

1 Cut the cardboard into squares to use as stamps.

2 To create different textures, glue cut pieces of craft foam to the cardboard squares, or wrap pipe cleaners around them (to make stripes, for example).

3 Pour a small amount of paint of various colors onto the baking sheet and spread it out a bit. Dip the stamps into the paint, using the same color each time for a given stamp. Start stamping a pattern by alternating the stamps in different colors and textures.

4 Continue stamping until you've filled the entire sheet of paper.

Who Knew??

You can get such great textures and patterns from cardboard, craft foam, and pipe cleaners!

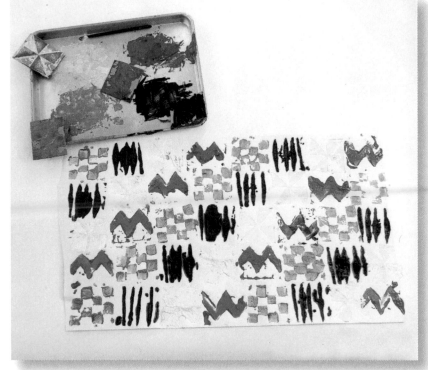

Buddhist Sand Pendulum Art

Buddhist monks create beautiful and intricate designs using colored sand. They begin by drawing geometric designs, then apply the sand using small tubes and funnels. Each design represents the universe and the teachings of their faith. The making of these designs is a sacred ritual and a form of meditation. Although this pendulum project is done differently, it's inspired by their work.

Math in Action: *counting, symmetry, time*

What You'll Need

empty water bottle with a flip top

single-hole punch

camera tripod or 3 wooden dowels to make one

yarn

colored sand

1 Cut off the bottom 2 inches (5 cm) of an empty water bottle. Use a hole punch to punch three holes evenly around the bottom edge of the cut bottle. Tie three pieces of yarn into the holes.

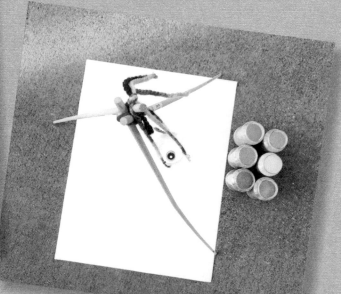

2 Build your tripod by tying together three wooden dowels (or use a premade tripod). Tie the water bottle pendulum to the tripod.

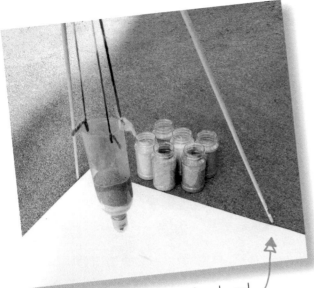

3 Fill the bottle with colored sand. Layer colors to make it more colorful!

4 Uncap the water bottle and start the bottle swinging.

5 Observe the swing and the movement of the pendulum and discuss the size of the patterns created. Measure how long it takes to empty the bottle of sand. How long does each swing last?

Spanish Geometric Tile Cube Puzzles

Spanish tiles, known as *azulejos*, are famous not only for their design, but also their function. You can find them in churches, palaces, schools, and even ordinary homes. The name originates from a word meaning "polished stone." They were originally made to represent the mosaics in Rome and Arabian countries. The tiles usually have interlocking lines, geometric shapes, and flowers. When they're assembled, they form amazing mosaics of colors and patterns! In this activity, you can create your own Spanish tile-inspired puzzle made from wooden cubes.

Math in Action: *geometry, symmetry*

What You'll Need

nine wooden cubes

paint

pictures of Spanish tiles, online or printed

1 Design and paint one side of each of the nine cubes with the same pattern and colors. You can look at pictures of Spanish tiles for inspiration.

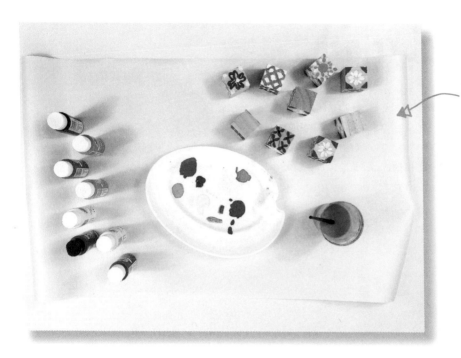

2 Turn the cubes and paint another side of each cube with another design.

3 Continue to paint all of six sides of the cubes, each set with a new design.

4 Now try matching up all the sides to play!

Ancient Cretan Labyrinth

If you've ever read any Greek mythology, you may know the story of the minotaur and the labyrinth. A labyrinth is like a maze, but it only has one spiraling path to the center. In a traditional labyrinth pattern, the traveler reverses directions nine times through eight rings with the pattern of left-right-outward-inward. It's easier than you think to draw your own labyrinth.

Math in Action: *counting, patterns, problem solving*

What You'll Need

paper

pencil

polymer clay

toothpick

marble or small ball

small clay knife (optional)

oven

acrylic paint

finishing glaze for clay (optional)

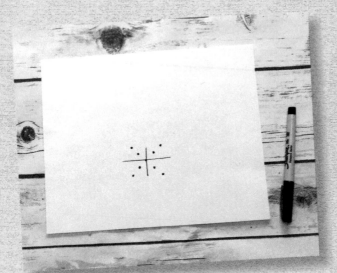

1 Draw your labyrinth. Start with an X of nine dots. Draw vertical and horizontal lines through the center dot. Draw vertical and horizontal rays from the next dots out, creating corners around the outermost dots, as shown.

2 Draw a curve from the top center line to the one just to the right.

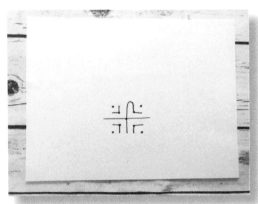

3 From the top of the top, left line, draw a curved line to the dot in the upper right. From the dot on the upper left, draw a curved line up and around the first line.

4 Continue in this pattern, moving counterclockwise to each point or line until you complete the design.

5 Repeat this design in clay. Roll out a circle of clay that's about ½ inch (1.25 cm) thick and 8 to 10 inches (20–25 cm) in diameter. Carve your pattern into the clay. The easiest way I've found to make the design in clay is pressing a marble around it. You could also carve it with a small clay knife. Bake the clay according to the package directions.

6 Once the clay is hardened, paint the path of the maze. Cover with a finishing glaze if desired. Follow the maze with your finger or a marble.

Try This!

Discover the mathematical patterns in the labyrinth. Number the labyrinth paths from top to bottom starting with 0 on the outside and down through 8. Now when you walk through the labyrinth you will follow this sequence: 0, 3, 2, 1, 4, 7, 6, 5, 8. What patterns can you discover? Can you draw a different style of labyrinth using the same technique?

Islamic Eight-Pointed Stars

In the Middle Ages, Islamic art began to feature an eight-pointed star or an octagram. In Arabic it's called the *Rub el Hizb*. It's used in the *Quran*, the holy book of Islam, to mark the end of each chapter. The pattern can be seen in mosques around the world. This eight-pointed star can be made easily by overlapping two squares of the same size, with one turned at an angle, making eight points.

Math in Action: *geometry, symmetry*

What You'll Need

large, white paper

pencil

scissors

glue, optional

oil pastels or other art medium

1 Begin by making a template for the eight-pointed star. Cut out two squares of the same size and overlap them. Turn one at an angle to make the eight points. You can glue these two together or trace them to make a one-piece template.

2 Trace the shape onto a piece of paper. Repeat, leaving a space between each shape that is the same width. This creates the X shape between each one. Continue drawing shapes until the page is filled.

3 Using one set of colors for all the eight-pointed stars and another set for all the X shapes, begin outlining and coloring in the shapes.

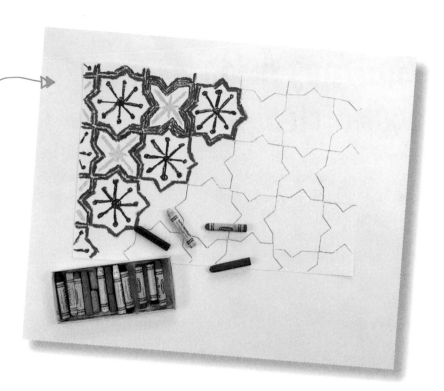

4 Complete your design by coloring all the shapes.

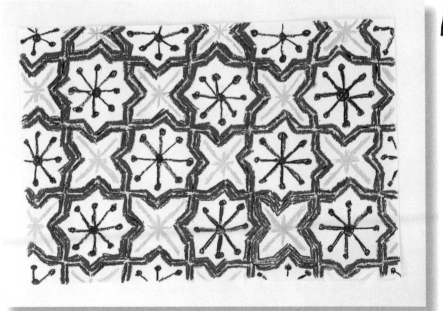

You can also trace square sticky notes to make your stars.

Yin-Yang Asian Geometrical Art

Yin and yang have been around since 200 BCE (before common era); they come from ancient Chinese religion and philosophy. The dark and the light parts of the yin-yang symbol are opposites that complement each other. They have equal areas. In Chinese philosophy, the two together bring balance. Yin, the black section, represents dark, cold, feminine, softness, and even numbers. Yang, the white section, represents light, warm, male, hardness, and odd numbers.

Math in Action: *geometry, shape*

What You'll Need
paper

compass

pencil

ruler

markers

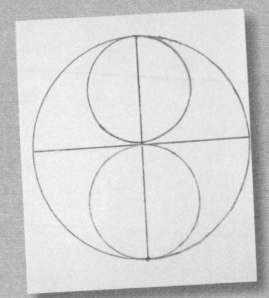

1 Draw a large circle in the center of your paper with a compass. Divide that circle in half both directions. Draw a smaller circle in the top and bottom halves as shown. Write lightly with your pencil, because you will be erasing many of these lines.

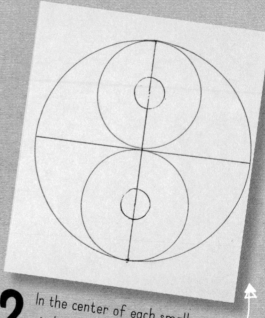

2 In the center of each small circle, draw another small circle.

3 Erase the cross lines and one side of each circle on opposite sides to make the yin-yang symbol.

4 Make a design out of your symbol. Try turning it into two whales.

5 Color in your design. Get creative and try others—any design you can think of. A night and day is another good option.

Try This!

Learn to draw your own yin-yang symbol. Then use your artistic ability to make it into something else!

6

Edible Math Art

One of my favorite ways to explore math is through baking. If you want to learn to cook, you need to know fractions and addition or subtraction for doubling and halving recipes. You also need to understand temperatures and thermometers. Also, did you know that cooking is an art form? You can create so much beauty through the food you prepare.

When you combine multiple senses in your learning, you will remember it more. So, enjoy eating your way through learning!

Pattern Block Cookies

Learning is always more fun when food—especially cookies—is involved! These pattern block cookies are exciting to make, use for math patterns, and eat.

Math in Action: *counting, fractions, geometry, measurement, patterns, shapes, spatial ability*

What You'll Need
COOKIES:

1 cup (225 g) butter

1 cup (200 g) granulated sugar

3 cups (375 g) all-purpose flour

1 egg

¾ teaspoon salt

1½ teaspoons (7 ml) vanilla extract

1 teaspoon (4 g) baking powder

1 tablespoon (15 ml) milk

Cookie cutters in geometric shapes (square, triangle, diamond, hexagon)

Wire cooling racks

Rimmed baking sheet

ICING:

2 pounds (0.9 kg, or about 7½ cups) powdered sugar

¾ cup (178 ml) milk or water

¾ cup (178 ml) corn syrup

2 teaspoons (10 ml) vanilla extract

Gel food coloring

1 Combine butter and sugar in the large bowl of an electric mixer. Add remaining ingredients through extract and mix well on low. Wrap dough in wax paper and refrigerate for about 1 hour.

2 Preheat oven to 350°F (180°C or gas mark 4). Roll out dough to about ¼-inch (6 mm) thickness. Use geometric-shaped cookie cutters to cut out shapes. Transfer shapes to ungreased baking sheet.

3 Bake for 8 to 10 minutes. Cool for 5 minutes. Transfer cookies to wire cooling racks to cool completely.

4 Make the icing: With an electric mixer, mix sugar and milk until smooth at a low speed. Stir in corn syrup and extract. Divide into 5 bowls and stir in food coloring to color each bowl separately.

5 Place the wire rack of cookies on a baking sheet. Pour icing over the cookies. Let the icing dry until hardened, about 12 hours.

6 Arrange the cookies to make geometric shapes and patterns.

Waffle Fraction Patterns

Waffles are the perfect food to use when learning about fractions. They already have sections, so it's easy to divide them up! In this edible math project, you can use waffles to create fractions and decorate each section with different yummy toppings.

Math in Action: *counting, fractions, measurement*

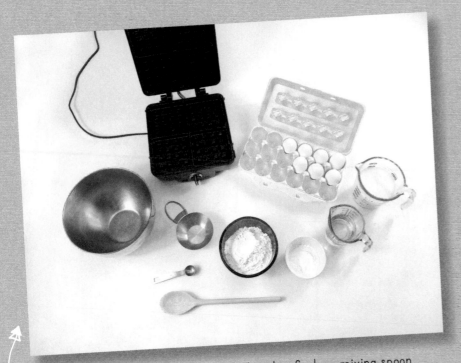

1 Beat eggs and milk in a large bowl with a fork or mixing spoon. Add remaining ingredients through the vanilla extract and mix until smooth.

What You'll Need

2 eggs

1¾ cups (414 ml) milk

2 cups (256 g) all-purpose flour

½ cup (118 ml) vegetable oil

1 tablespoon (14 g) baking powder

1 tablespoon (12 g) granulated sugar

¼ teaspoon salt

1 teaspoon (5 ml) vanilla extract

nonstick cooking spray for waffle iron

waffle toppings (berries, syrup, chocolate chips, and whipped cream)

2 Preheat a waffle iron and spray it with cooking spray. Cook batter in the waffle iron until waffles are lightly golden.

Eat Your Math Homework

After you divide up your toppings into sections, reward yourself by taking a bite out of it!

3 Cut waffles into various fractions and decorate sections with waffle toppings. Use math to determine the area covered by each topping. Enjoy!

Chocolate Square Splatter Art

Who doesn't love a delicious square of chocolate? This artistic project will make your chocolate beautiful to look at, and it's a blast!

Math in Action: *counting, fractions, percentages*

What You'll Need

colored chocolate wafers

chocolate molds

chocolate (white and milk or dark)

1 Melt each color of chocolate in a separate bowl, following the package directions. Eight different colors of wafers were used in the example, but you can choose any number of colors you want for your design.

2 Using a spoon, drizzle each color across the chocolate molds.

3 Melt regular and white chocolate in the microwave in separate microwave-safe bowls in 30-second increments, stirring each time. Pour over the top of the colored patterns, filling the rest of the molds.

4 Let cool and remove from molds.

5 Count how many squares show each color that you used. Calculate the fractions and percentages for each.

Bread Art: Doubling a Recipe

There's a lot of math involved in baking. In this project, practice your math skills by doubling a recipe. Then share your product! This recipe makes artisan rolls that are crispy on the outside and soft and chewy on the inside. You can form your rolls into all kinds of shapes to make beautiful bread art.

Math in Action: *addition, fractions*

What You'll Need

1 teaspoon (3.5 g) yeast

2 cups (473 ml) warm water

4 cups (420 g) wheat or white flour, plus extra for flouring

2 teaspoons (10 g) salt

1 tablespoon (12 g) granulated sugar or 1 tablespoon (15 ml) honey

1 Activate the yeast in the warm water. In the large mixing bowl of an electric mixer, mix together flour, salt, yeast, and sugar on medium until a dough forms. Cover with a lid or towel and let rest about 2 hours. It will still be sticky and somewhat bubbly after rising.

2 Preheat oven to 425°F (220°C or gas mark 7). Spread flour on a counter and divide the dough into twelve to sixteen equal pieces. Form pieces into a variety of small shapes. If the dough is sticky, roll it in a little more flour. Place the dough shapes on a lightly greased pan and let rise for another 20 minutes. Bake for 15 to 20 minutes, until lightly golden.

3 Want to share your bread? Try using your math skills to double this recipe. Then take some to a friend.

Stained Glass Gelatin Art

This colorful, edible project is both delicious and beautiful. Plus, you can learn your way through eating.

Math in Action: *counting, fractions, measurement*

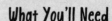

What You'll Need

Five or six 3-ounce (85 g) boxes of different colors of gelatin

Cooking spray

Two 2½ teaspoon (11 g) packets unflavored gelatin

One 14-ounce (396 g) can sweetened condensed milk

1 Make each type of gelatin in a separate bowl, following package directions. Grease a square or rectangular pan for each color using cooking spray. Pour each color into a pan to chill.

2 Once the gelatin is chilled, cut it into small cubes. Gently place all colors together in one large 9 × 13 (23 × 33 cm) pan.

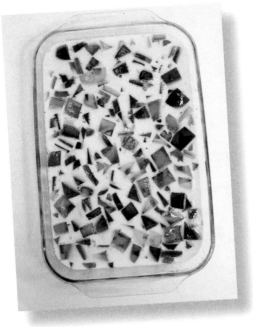

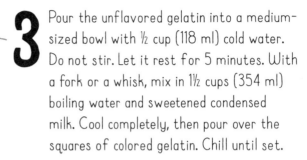

3 Pour the unflavored gelatin into a medium-sized bowl with ½ cup (118 ml) cold water. Do not stir. Let it rest for 5 minutes. With a fork or a whisk, mix in 1½ cups (354 ml) boiling water and sweetened condensed milk. Cool completely, then pour over the squares of colored gelatin. Chill until set.

4 Cut into squares and serve.

5 Count the number of squares of each color you see in your piece of gelatin. Total them up and turn them into fractions. For instance, if you see fourteen different squares of color and three of them are red, your piece is ³/₁₄ red.

How Many Squares of Color?

Red	Orange	Yellow	Green	Blue
8	10	4	3	3

Templates

On the next few pages are some templates that you can use to complete various activties in this book. Feel free to copy and enlarge the templates when you use them.

Skip Counting Circular Art (see project on page 38)

Dot Art Grid (see project on page 34)

Hundred Square Chart (see project on page 44)

Kirigami Cutting Template: Circle (see project on page 54)

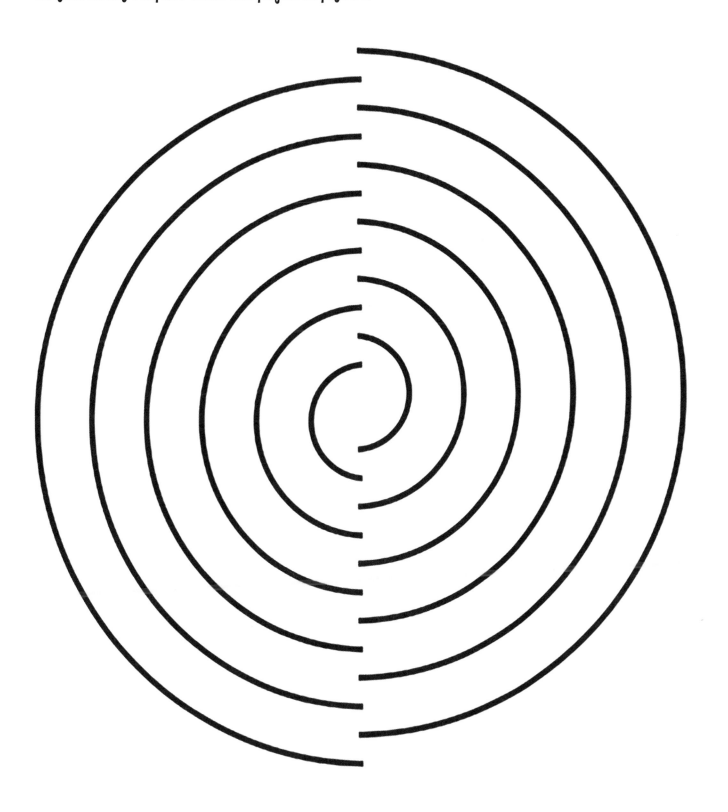

Kirigami Cutting Template: Hexagon (see project on page 54)

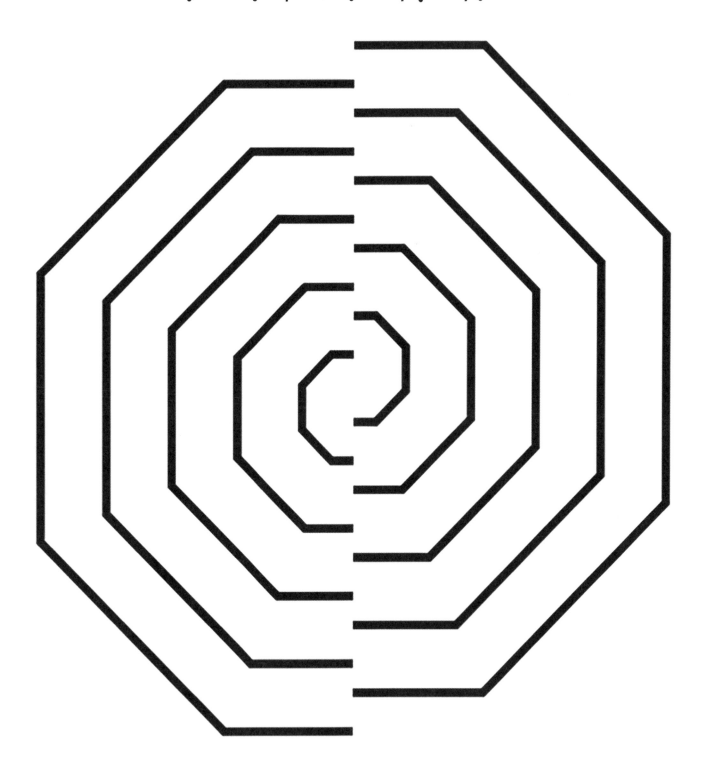

Kirigami Cutting Template: Square (see project on page 54)

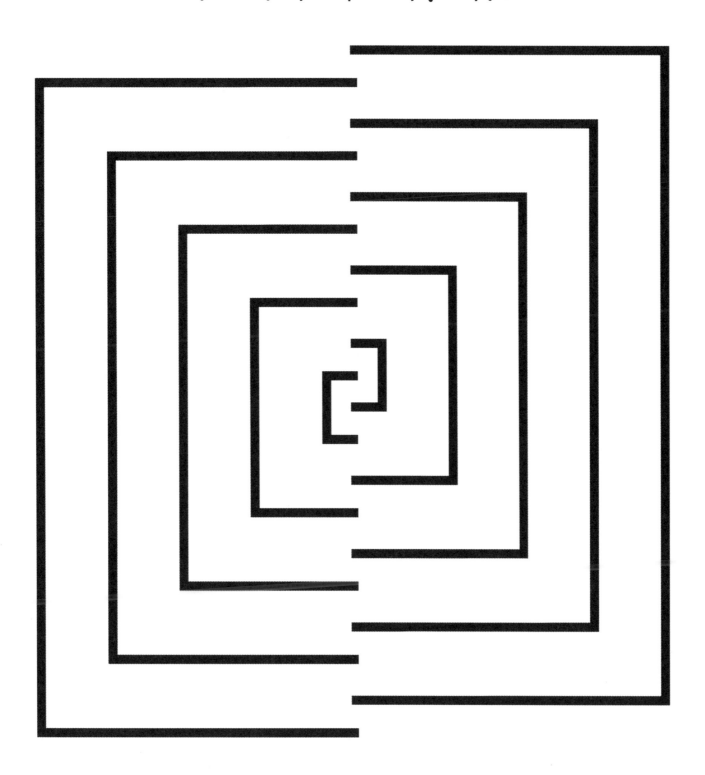

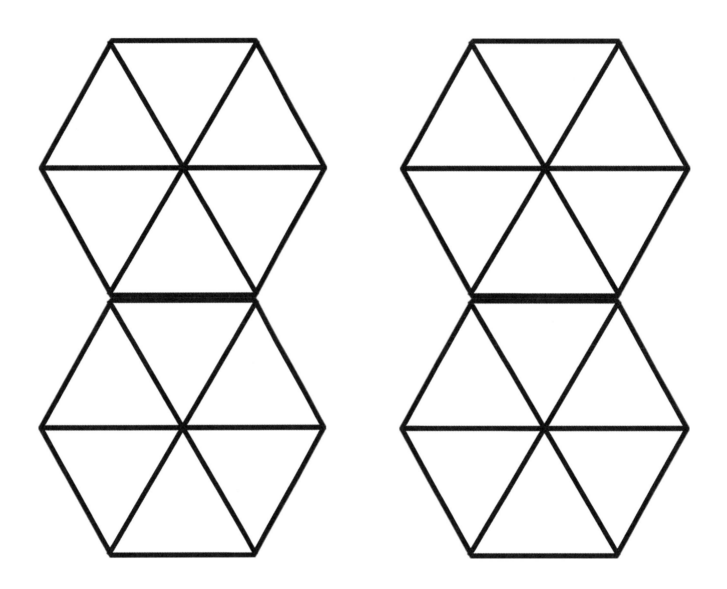

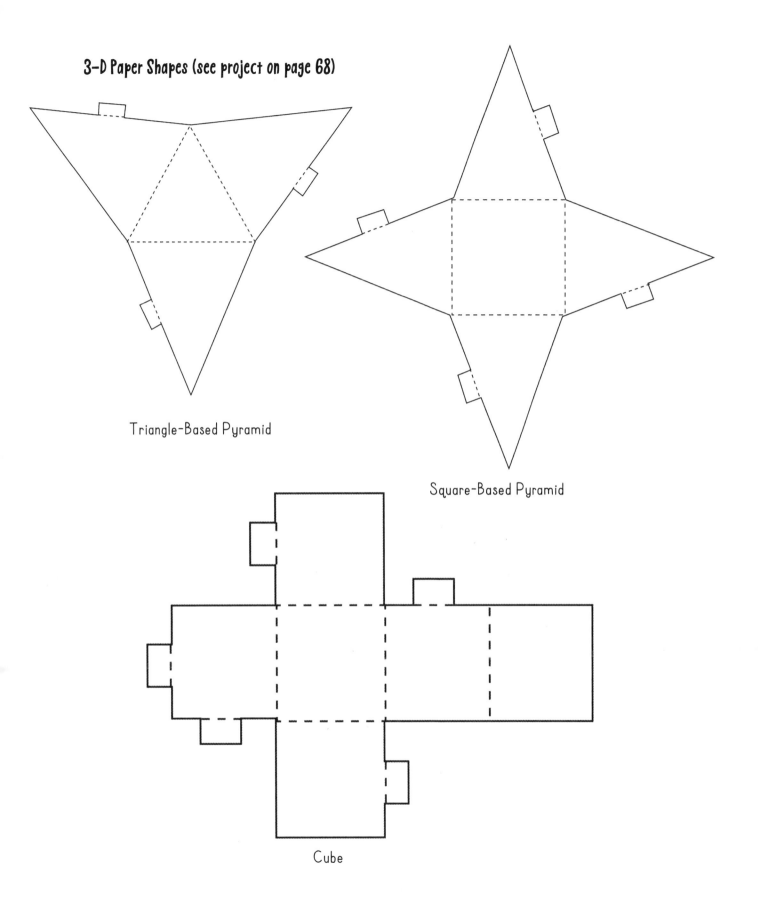

3-D Paper Shapes (see project on page 68)

Triangle-Based Pyramid

Square-Based Pyramid

Cube

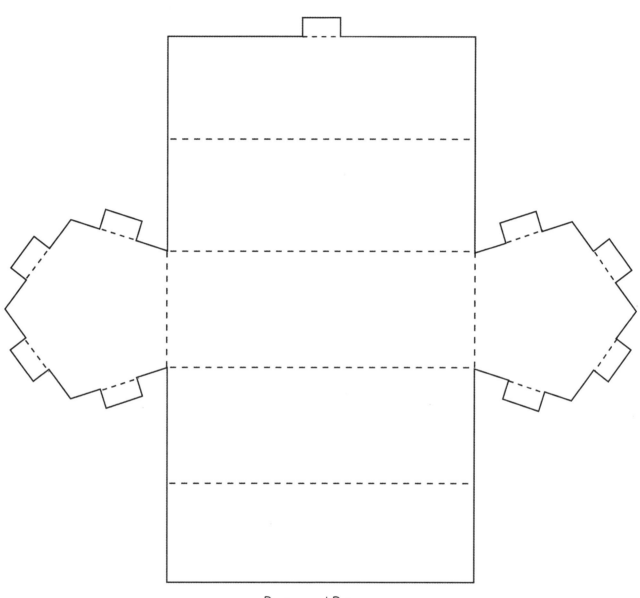

Pentagonal Prism

3-D Paper Shapes (see project on page 68)

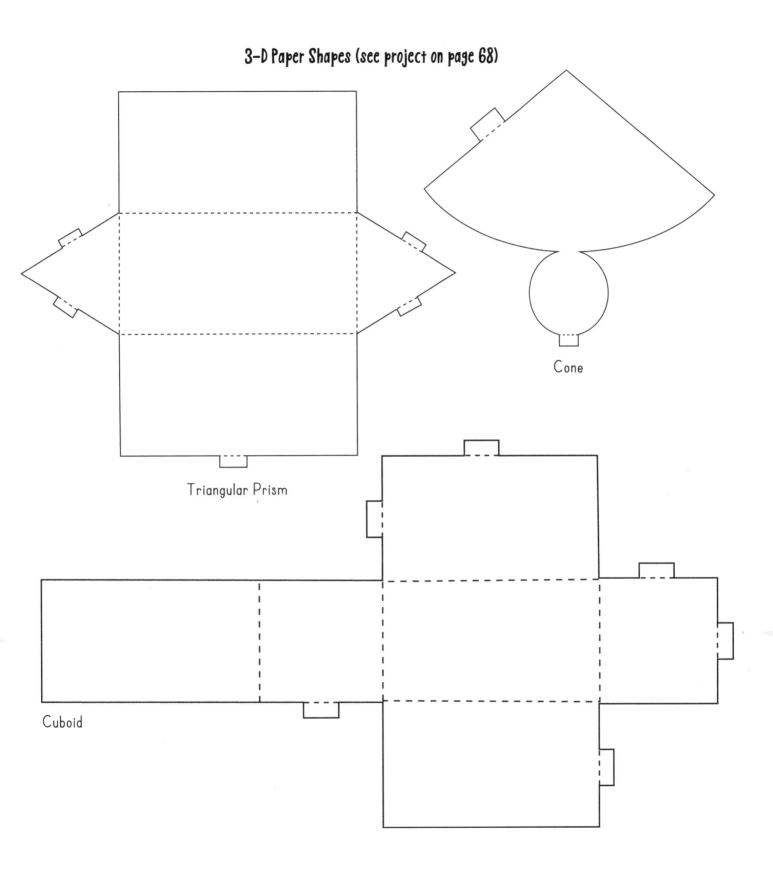

Triangular Prism

Cone

Cuboid

3-D Paper Shapes (see project on page 68)

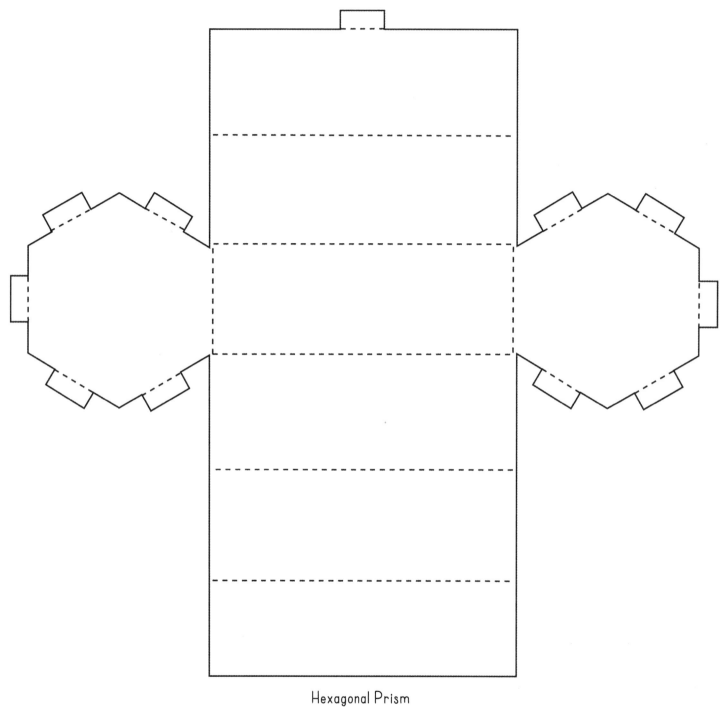

Hexagonal Prism

Resources

Most of the supplies in this book are easy to acquire at any store in the craft section. I shop online to buy in bulk and to search for the hard-to-find supplies. For geometric cookie cutters for the Pattern Block Cookies (page 90), check etsy.com.

Learn more about the artists in this book:

Museum of Modern Art: moma.org/artists
Alexander Calder: calder.org
M. C. Escher: mcescher.com
Jasper Johns: jasper-johns.org
Vasily Kandinsky: wassilykandinsky.net
Paul Klee: paulklee.net
Piet Mondrian: piet-mondrian.org
Frank Stella: artnet.com/artists/frank-stella
Victor Vasarely: artnet.com/artists/victor-vasarely
Frank Lloyd Wright: franklloydwright.org

Learn more about ancient art from around the world:

Artsy: artsy.net/gene/ancient-art
Metropolitan Museum of Art: metmuseum.org/toah/chronology

About the Author

KARYN TRIPP is a former public-school teacher turned homeschool mom of four kids. Through her online community TeachBesideMe.com, she shares with teachers and homeschool parents how to make learning enjoyable and engaging, and she eases the burdens of her fellow educators by offering exciting and memorable learning activities. Karyn is also a member of STEAM Kids Books, a group of educational bloggers—engineers, teachers, math nerds, art lovers, and writers—who have cowritten and self-published three titles. She lives in Utah.

Index

A

addition
    Bread Art: Doubling a Recipe, 96–97
    Golden Spiral Art, 40–41
    introduction, 11
    Skip Counting Circular Art, 38–39
    Square Numbers Tower, 32–33
    Triangle Math Puzzle, 66–67
    Vedic Square, 44–45
angles
    Descending Polygons, 64–65
    Frank Lloyd Wright's Geometric
        Stained-Glass Art, 28–29
    Frank Stella's Protractor Art,
        24–25
    introduction, 11
area
    Descending Polygons, 64–65
    Dot Grid Art, 34–35
    introduction, 11
    Multiplication Grid Art, 36–37
    Square Numbers Tower, 32–33

B

balance
    Alexander Calder's Face Mobile,
        22–23
    introduction, 11

C

concentric circles
    introduction, 11
    Kirigami Paper Cutting, 54–55
coordinate planes, 11
counting
    Ancient Cretan Labyrinth, 82–83
    Buddhist Sand Pendulum Art, 78–79
    Chocolate Square Splatter Art,
        94–95
    Dot Grid Art, 34–35
    introduction, 11
    Jasper Johns's Hidden Number Art,
        26–27
    Multiplication Grid Art, 36–37
    Paper Clip Symmetrical Art, 50–51
    Pattern Block Cookies, 90–91
    Stained Glass Gelatin Art, 98–99
    Waffle Fraction Patterns, 92–93

D

diameter of a circle, 11
dimensions
    Alexander Calder's Face Mobile,
        22–23
    introduction, 11

F

fractions
    Bread Art: Doubling a Recipe, 96–97
    Chocolate Square Splatter Art, 94–95
    introduction, 11
    Pattern Block Cookies, 90–91
    Stained Glass Gelatin Art, 98–99
    Waffle Fraction Patterns, 92–93

G

geometry
    3-D Paper Shapes, 68–69
    African Kente-Pattern Prints,
        76–77
    Descending Polygons, 64–65
    Dot Grid Art, 34–35
    Frank Lloyd Wright's Geometric
        Stained-Glass Art, 28–29
    Frank Stella's Protractor Art,
        24–25
    Golden Spiral Art, 40–41
    introduction, 11
    Islamic Eight-Pointed Stars, 84–85
    Kirigami Paper Cutting, 54–55
    Mandala Drawings, 52–53
    M. C. Escher's Infinity Triangles,
        18–19
    Native American Quill Art, 74–75
    Pattern Block Cookies, 90–91
    Paul Klee's Geometric Mosaic, 16–17
    Rose Window Stained Glass, 56–57
    Rotational Symmetry, 48–49
    Spanish Geometric Tile Cube
        Puzzles, 80–81
    Spiral Squares, 62–63
    Tetrahedral Kite, 70–71
    Triangle Math Puzzle, 66–67
    Vedic Square, 44–45
    Victor Vasarely's Op Art Illusions,
        20–21
    Yin-Yang Asian Geometrical Art,
        86–87
golden ratio
    Golden Spiral Art, 40–41
    introduction, 12
graphs, 12

I

isosceles triangle
    introduction, 12
    M. C. Escher's Infinity Triangles,
        18–19

M

measurement
    Descending Polygons, 64–65
    Frank Stella's Protractor Art,
        24–25
    Hectograph Ink Prints, 58–59
    introduction, 12
    M. C. Escher's Infinity Triangles,
        18–19
    Native American Quill Art, 74–75
    Pattern Block Cookies, 90–91
    Spiral Squares, 62–63
    Splash Patterns, 42–43

Stained Glass Gelatin Art, 98–99
    Tetrahedral Kite, 70–71
    Waffle Fraction Patterns, 92–93
multiplication
    Golden Spiral Art, 40–41
    introduction, 12
    Multiplication Grid Art, 36–37
    Skip Counting Circular Art, 38–39
    Square Numbers Tower, 32–33
    Triangle Math Puzzle, 66–67
    Vedic Square, 44–45

N

negative numbers, 12
number recognition
    introduction, 12
    Jasper Johns's Hidden Number Art,
        26–27

P

parallel lines
    Frank Lloyd Wright's Geometric
        Stained-Glass Art, 28–29
    introduction, 12
    Kirigami Paper Cutting, 54–55
    Victor Vasarely's Op Art Illusions,
        20–21
patterns
    African Kente-Pattern Prints,
        76–77
    Ancient Cretan Labyrinth, 82–83
    Frank Lloyd Wright's Geometric
        Stained-Glass Art, 28–29
    introduction, 12
    Pattern Block Cookies, 90–91
    Paul Klee's Geometric Mosaic, 16–17
    Vedic Square, 44–45
percentage
    Chocolate Square Splatter Art,
        94–95
    introduction, 12
    Vedic Square, 44–45
perimeter
    Descending Polygons, 64–65
    Dot Grid Art, 34–35
    introduction, 12
    Square Numbers Tower, 32–33
perpendicular lines
    Frank Lloyd Wright's Geometric
        Stained-Glass Art, 28–29
    introduction, 12
    Kirigami Paper Cutting, 54–55
pi, 12
positive numbers, 12
problem solving
    Ancient Cretan Labyrinth, 82–83
    introduction, 12
proportion
    Alexander Calder's Face Mobile,
        22–23
    introduction, 12

R

right triangle
    introduction, 12
    M. C. Escher's Infinity Triangles,
        18–19

S

shape
    3-D Paper Shapes, 68–69
    Hectograph Ink Prints, 58–59
    introduction, 12
    Pattern Block Cookies, 90–91
    Rose Window Stained Glass, 56–57
    Spiral Squares, 62–63
    Tetrahedral Kite, 70–71
    Victor Vasarely's Op Art Illusions,
        20–21
    Yin-Yang Asian Geometrical Art,
        86–87
skip counting
    introduction, 13
    Skip Counting Circular Art, 38–39
spatial ability
    introduction, 13
    Pattern Block Cookies, 90–91
    Paul Klee's Geometric Mosaic, 16–17
subtraction, 13
symmetry
    African Kente-Pattern Prints,
        76–77
    Alexander Calder's Face Mobile,
        22–23
    Buddhist Sand Pendulum Art, 78–79
    Hectograph Ink Prints, 58–59
    introduction, 13
    Islamic Eight-Pointed Stars, 84–85
    Mandala Drawings, 52–53
    Native American Quill Art, 74–75
    Paper Clip Symmetrical Art, 50–51
    Rose Window Stained Glass, 56–57
    Rotational Symmetry, 48–49
    Spanish Geometric Tile Cube
        Puzzles, 80–81

T

temperature, 13
templates
    3-D Paper Shapes, 107, 108, 109, 110
    Dot Art Grid, 101
    Hundred Square Chart, 102
    Kirigami Paper Cutting, 103, 104, 105
    Skip Counting Circular Art, 100
    Triangle Math Puzzle, 106
time
    Buddhist Sand Pendulum Art, 78–79
    introduction, 13

W

weight
    Alexander Calder's Face Mobile,
        22–23
    introduction, 13